ACKNO

CW01499585

The following book could not have been written without the input of the GHOSTnortheast team and their commitment to spending every other weekend hunting for ghosts and then sending me their reports.

To the originals; Lynne Ellison, James Turnbull and Mandy Howland, who were there from day one. Karen Mann, Catherine Murphy, Natalie Jones, Michael Anderson, Leanne Day who have helped us on our way.

To the current team of Peter Woolford, Marty Winch Danielle Taylor, Chris Wall, Paul Hannon and Yvette Watson.

And not forgetting Angela Watson and David Howland who with myself, have been here for the past seven years.

I must also thank all the locations and their employees who have trusted and helped us on our investigations. But most of all I must thank you the "Ghosties" whether it's attending one of our nights or talking to us on Facebook. Whatever your contribution over the years, it is you guys that make our group so enjoyable and successful.

STEVE WATSON

I had entered the gents toilet prior to knowing of the strangling sensation, I didn't feel such sensation but something felt odd

GHOSTnortheast

The Chronicles of

A Ghost Hunter

Volume 1

By

Steve Watson

ISBN 1976396581
ISBN-13: 978-1976396588

STEVE WATSON

DEDICATION

THIS BOOK IS DEDICATED TO MY
BEAUTIFUL WIFE ANGELA,
MY TWO FANTASTIC SONS DANIEL
AND JOE AND MY TWO GORGEOUS
LITTLE GRANDDAUGHTERS FAITH
AND SCARLETT. WITHOUT THEIR
LOVE AND SUPPORT THIS BOOK
WOULD HAVE NEVER SEEN THE
LIGHT OF DAY!!

STEVE WATSON

CONTENTS

1 INTRODUCTION

I became interested in the paranormal over 30 years ago, as a teenager growing up in Northumberland. I encountered something extremely strange in a place called Arcot Hall in a small town called Cramlington. To this day I still don't know if I imagined the figure I saw, or if it was something that could have a perfectly reasonable explanation. I do know it terrified me and I have never ran as fast I did that day.

I then spent many school holidays and winter evenings in the local library reading everything I could about the paranormal, local legends and ghost stories. I would often tune into our local radio station at night time to listen to a program called "Alan Robson's Night Owls." This would be full of locals ringing in to tell their own ghostly encounters and debate the existence of the afterlife. I remember listening to Alan's live ghost hunts, pulling my legs closer to my chest and pulling the blanket over my head with my heart racing as he took us on these frightening adventures.

As the years passed, the paranormal took a backseat when I began working and raising my family. But the passion was relit with the introduction of programs such as Most Haunted. My wife and I would sit for hours watching these TV programs and at the same time I dusted down the covers of my old book collection. As my children grew older, my wife and I joined a few group hunts in and around Newcastle with our friends David and Mandy Howland. However, we couldn't seem to settle with a group as they either concentrated too much on the psychic elements; were too focused on entertainment, or were too serious and scientific.

David and I were returning from a trip from York when we decided we should open our own group. We wanted to be 100% genuine and 100% honest. If nothing happened, then nothing happened. But, if we did see, feel or hear things then we knew as far as we were concerned that the activity would be real. We wouldn't use Mediums or Psychics but we would mix scientific experiments with psychic tools such as Ouija Boards. So, GHOSTnortheast was born and seven years later, we are bigger and more popular than ever! It just goes to show honesty is the best policy.

The following book is based on the reports from some of our most active locations. I have included a history of the locations we investigate, and I have tried my best to write in a chronological format so you can see how much of the activity we documented is repeated.

I do hope you enjoy reading it as much as I have enjoyed hunting over the past seven years. And I do hope it makes you think about what we have encountered. If you find you get bitten by the bug, don't forget you can always join us on a hunt and become a paranormal investigator for yourself.

Enjoy!

STEVE WATSON

2 TOOLS OF THE TRADE

Before we get started on the actual investigations, I need to explain some of the equipment we use. As you read through the reports, you will come across references to various pieces of equipment that we use during our investigations. I have tried to include as many pieces of equipment as possible in the following pages.

PSYCHIC TOOLS:

Ouija Boards:

Love it or hate it the Ouija Board is still the biggest talking point of any investigation. Some people can't wait to get their hands on it, while others will not even stand in the same room as one. But why have they caused such a stir in our culture?

The Ouija is also known as a Talking Board or Spirit Board. The name is believed to derive from the French and the German for "Yes". However, there are other claims that it originates from an old Egyptian word for good luck. The origin of the board and the name seems to be as mysterious as the object itself.

Although used in the 19th Century, it wasn't until July 1st, 1890 that the first commercial Board became available. It was marketed in the US by businessman Elijah Bond, who stated that Ouija was a harmless parlour game to play with friends and family. The link to the occult doesn't seem to appear until it's use by spiritualist Pearl Curran in the early 1900s.

In 1966, ownership passed to Parker Brothers who continued to sell it as a simple family game where it sat on toyshop shelves next to Monopoly and Scrabble. Today, the patent is owned by Hasbro. So how does a simple toy strike fear into the hearts of many of its players?

The consistent use of the boards during séances in Victorian times always gave it the element of intrigue. However, in later years Hollywood began to use it as a key tool in raising devils and demons in its horror blockbusters. In 1973 the release of "The Exorcist" created a string of urban myths about how using the board could open the door to hell and lead to you being possessed.

Immediately, there were calls by religious groups to stop the sale of such a satanic object. But still there was no evidence to suggest that the board did anything other than entertain its participants.

The Psychic belief revolves around contact with the spirit world. Believers call out and ask questions of any spirits around them that may want to communicate. They believe that the spirit then comes forward and controls the glass or Planchette to spell out it's answers and get its message across to the living world.

Believers of the board are extremely wary of using the board by themselves or in uncontrolled conditions with the fear of hostile or evil forces coming through. The board is to be blessed before the session and then closed properly at the end. This protects the users. During the Victorian era of Mediumship, Mediums would surround the board with food and wine to encourage spirits to come forward and talk to the room.

Now, the scientific belief is quite different and is based on the human brains' ability to make movements without registering them. There has been extensive research on this theory by various scientists and psychologists who insist there is nothing sinister in the board at all. Their belief is that the boards' response is down to the "operator" as the person using the board is known and a term known as "ideomotor response" or "The Carpenter Effect."
This theory dates to 1852 when William Benjamin Carpenter studied Ouija Boards along with table tipping, dowsing and automatic writing that was being displayed by mediums at the time. His theory was the brain could react without the person involved having to make a conscious effort, in a similar way to modern day hypnosis. The problem is the same as the

paranormal belief, with tests still showing as inconclusive.

The final belief is that the movement of the Ouija is simply, someone pushing the glass. As an investigation team we try and take every precaution to eliminate this happening; for example, turning fingers upside down so it is more difficult to control the glass and having guests taking their fingers off the glass one at a time. But again, it leaves us without an answer either way.

The Ouija will always be the most controversial of devices used by a paranormal group as there is no way of proving its authenticity. However, over the years of using it on various locations, I still scratch my head at some of the responses it has given. I have been present when the glass was moving around the table anti-clockwise but the glass itself was spinning clockwise as it moved. I have not been able to replicate this motion just using my fingertips.

I have also witnessed two groups of totally unrelated people who had no contact with each other at all; yet both groups responses spelled out the exact same answers. I cannot guarantee it wasn't paranormal, but I also cannot say it was. I do know I could not explain it when asked about it afterwards, by the people taking part. Even reflecting on the evidence as I look back, I'm still confused as to what went on.

So, whether the board is fear, fun or fake, we believe it is down to the belief of the users. There have been no demonic or negative consequences for the team or any of our guests using the board. It's said that a sceptic will never accept the word of a believer and the believer will spend their time trying to convince the sceptic. Therefore, in true GHOSTnortheast style, we will leave you to decide!

I'll move on by explaining The Planchette, Pendulum Crystals and Dowsing Rods. We have grouped them together as they are recognised as items of divination and we often refer to them as our psychic tools rather than the scientific equipment that we use.

The Planchette:

The Planchette we use is a piece of wood on wheels with a pen through the centre. This is then put onto a sheet of paper. The investigators then put their fingers on it, and wait for a spirit to move it around spelling words or drawing pictures to contact the users. This is also known as "Automatic Writing".

The Planchette responds like the Ouija Board when used in a group. But where the Ouija has been portrayed as an object of evil, never to be used alone, the Planchette doesn't have same reputation and is commonly used by a single person to contact the dead.

The earliest mention of the use of a Planchette dates back over 2000 years to ancient China. Although it looks different to its modern western version, it works in the exact same way.

The Chinese version used two branches of a tree as

handles held by the users and a third smaller branch was joined to create a pointer. This structure was placed in a sandpit, where the users would ask questions. The Chinese believed that a specific spirit or God would enter the Planchette and speak through it, whereas the Western belief is that the dead use it as a point of contact to the living.

The Western version doesn't seem to appear that often until Victorian times, when it was regarded as an essential part of a séance. It would be introduced by the Medium along with the Ouija Board to speak to the "other side". The Medium would close their eyes and place both hands on the Planchette and begin a callout. This is now better known as Automatic Writing.

GHOSTnortheast introduced the Planchette experiment in 2011 after we researched Victorian Séances, and over the years we have seen some impressive results. I recall a night at Chillingham Castle when we seemed to receive a picture of a man and the name "John" clearly written on the paper. This was drawn when a group of 3 people had their fingers upturned on the Planchette, and in total darkness. We have tried to replicate the drawings in the same conditions and must admit it was extremely difficult, very time consuming and we had to talk to each other so we all pushed the same way at the same time.

The psychic belief is that the Planchette works in the same way as a Ouija Board; a spirit uses the energy of its users to move the object around the paper to message the living world. The Scientific theory is more straightforward, it is simply being pushed by the users, with some saying that the user(s) may not even be aware that they are pushing it, as it being moved sub-consciously. However, there is still no process to prove either theory.

Crystal Pendulums:

These objects are probably one of the most used for divination and dowsing. They are simple to use and can be mastered quickly, and they are inexpensive and easy to source. Pendulums are used in various walks of life from Holistic Healers to Dowsers looking for water or Ley Lines.

The Pendulum itself is usually a symmetrically weighted object at the end of a chain. It can be any object that is not magnetic, but in our investigations, we use crystals. The user then holds the chain in their fingers and concentrates before asking questions. The Pendulum is then deemed to be a receiver and transmitter of information to answer the users' questions by a series of movements, usually announced at the start of a session. For example, swinging back and forth is a "Yes" and spinning in circles is a "No".

The psychic theory is that the pendulum is moved by spirits or a higher power that can use energy to move it as a means of contact. As the crystal is a natural element, it is more in tune with the natural energies of the Earth, making it easier for the spirit to move and give information.

The scientific theory is more straight forward (as with all divination tools), and they say it is moved by the user either consciously or subconsciously, manipulating it to give the answers they want to hear. Again, there is no process in place to prove either theory is right.

The Dowsing Rods:

It is believed that Dowsing with rods originates as early the 1500's and seems to have been first used in Germany to find metal. In 1518, it was listed as occultism by Martin Luther and is mentioned in many texts during the mid-1500s. The Rods are a relatively basic piece of equipment, early forms were usually made from tree branches that grew as a wishbone type shape. Later they changed to metal rods bent into a L shape.

Over the years, they were used to find water, metal, petrol or anything else in the ground of value.
The theory being that the shape of the rods can fine tune into energies to find what item you are looking for. In paranormal use, they are used to communicate with the dead by using movements to answer questions.

The scientific theory is that they merely amplify the movements of the user and are connected to the Ideomotor Effect. (The Ideomotor Effect is where the brain operates sub-consciously and will give reflexive responses like when the body is in pain.)

The scientific world has spent a lot of time and

money on researching Dowsing, with several scientific experiments based on recording the findings of Dowsers. Many of these experiments that have been conducted under controlled conditions have concluded that the Rods gave answers no better than chance. This gave scientists the belief that there is no evidence what so ever to suggest that Dowsing Rods are no more than a gimmick.

GHOSTnortheast has witnessed Dowsing Rods moving to request and movement answering various questions. Could this be coincidence or chance? Were the Rods simply amplifying the thoughts of the user? Again, we will let you decide!

SCIENTIFIC TOOLS:

The EMF and K-2 Meters:

To new guests they seem like little boxes with either a needle that makes funny noises, or a row of flashing lights. They often ask why most paranormal teams get a little excited with the rise and fall of the strange beeping and flashing. Here we will try an explain the workings and both the science and paranormal beliefs behind the Meters.

The Science:
EMF stands for Electro Magnetic Field. This is a physical field produced by electrically charged objects.

The EMF Meter measures the amount of charged particles in the surrounding area. These are measured in milligauss or "mg". The meter is used in everyday life (by mainly Electricians and Builders) to locate poorly insulated wiring or electrical sources. The meter is simple; the closer you are to an electrical source the higher the reading. These readings present as sounds, and as the electricity in circuits is constant, the sound on the meter will also be a non-fluctuating tone. The K-2 works in the same way but uses small light bulbs that shine green, amber and red to show how strong the current is.

For example, if you were to switch a lamp on and hold the meter close to the lamp, the meter will give you a constant read of EMF measurement. The meter will not stop recording reads until the lamp is switched off. But what has this got to do with ghosts?

The Paranormal:
It is believed in the paranormal world of investigation that ghosts create an electric current when trying to show themselves or interact. If this is true, then they would create an electromagnetic field as they changed and charged the surrounding particles. This is what the EMF reads.

The theory of the fluctuations is that the spirit is moving around to cause the spikes and lows. Remember, if it was a natural electric field, the device would not fluctuate but would be constant!

GHOSTnortheast walk around our locations before an investigation, and take ambient readings of EMF. We also note any natural areas of electricity that could influence the meter during the investigation, such as a boiler that might switch on during the night, or a timer switch on a light.

As we use older buildings we must be careful to note their normal readings, because in some locations there can be a naturally high reading. When this occurs, we don't use the equipment in that area. (The Castle Keep has a naturally high EMF read due to its proximity to the railway lines).

I will probably repeat what a lot of long serving paranormal investigators would say and that is some of the most impressive photographs, video footage and activity has been witnessed during and after an active EMF session. We have witnessed the meter go from 0mg to 10mg instantly on request only for it to fall back to 0mg when asked.

For example, in my experience, possibly the best location for EMF readings heralding activity is The Lit & Phil in Newcastle. In one location, we asked for the EMF to be affected. We have it recorded and have the video footage of it raising and falling to request. On this occasion, the additional vigils reported numerous contacts, with unexplained photographs and video footage.

However, we cannot rule out mere coincidence and at GHOSTnortheast we look at all possibilities. Science will say the meter is being affected by something quite natural as it is the only explanation, but paranormal believers will say it is a way for spirits to contact us.

The Frank's Box:

The Frank's Box is probably my favourite tool. It is a FM/AM radio with a scanning facility just like any normal radio in the home. The box has been altered so it constantly scans, unlike the one in your home which will stop when it finds a radio station.

The belief is that you scan the radio waves and the spirit or ghost will emphasise any words that they want to use to communicate with us, or stop the scan on specific messages. It was created by American Frank Sumption. This piece of equipment has become a must in any ghost hunters inventory. While you can listen live, the messages can be recorded and played back like an EVP. However, sceptics dismiss these words and messages as simple coincidence or pareidolia.

Thermometers:

We use two different thermometers to record temperatures throughout the investigations. We use a USB logger which measures the temperature of the room and is has real time readings showing us any fluctuations at the time. We also use a laser thermometer. This lets us record an accurate reading from a more precise area. For example, if someone is feeling difference in temperatures on their body or a cold spot, we can use the laser to point to the exact area.

Kaleidoscope Laser pointer:

This is a simple presentation laser pointer that has been modified. Instead of it only having one point of light, it disperses the light into many different points, allowing us to fill an entire area with small dots of light. We have had success with this experiment as people have reported movement and shadows in the matrix of dots.

Digital Voice Recorder:

DVRs or Dictaphones are a simple audio recording device. We use these to see if they record anything we may have missed on the night. These audio recordings are always known as Electronic Voice Phenomena or EVPs. I have heard many EVPs over the years and some I cannot explain.

STEVE WATSON

3 THE LIT AND PHIL
NEWCASTLE'S OLDEST LIBRARY

As Newcastle is the hometown of GHOSTnortheast, it is only fitting that we start our book at our spiritual home, the Lit & Phil, in the heart of the City. Located at the bottom of Westgate Road between the Central Station and Castle Keep in the centre of Newcastle Upon Tyne, this glorious 19th century Grade 2 listed building is the home to The Newcastle Literary and Philosophical Society.

The library is currently spread across 3 floors and houses the largest independent collection of literature and music outside of London.

The Society was founded in 1793 as a conservative club where the book subjects were wide ranging, but religion and politics were prohibited. The Society met up in various locations during this time, as the current building was yet to be built. It was very liberal for its day and admitted its first women members in 1804, although they still had their own reading area. In 1820, the Newcastle upon Tyne Society for the gradual abolition of Slavery in the British Dominions was formed within the building.

The Society was also a very innovative institution, and new technologies were often displayed to its members including George Stephenson with his Miners lamp in 1815. Later, The Lit&Phil became the first public building ever to be lit by electric light when Joseph Swan arrived in 1880 with his latest invention - the light bulb.

During the 19th and 20th centuries the Society also branched out into music and lectures. Some notable names to speak here included Oscar Wilde, Mary Kingsley and your very own GHOSTnortheast!
Since 1895 The Society has kept a list of its members, and it reads like a Who's Who of The North East with such names as WG Armstrong, Thomas Bewick, Richard Grainger and Neil Tennant of The Pet Shop Boys. The Society is still an active lending library and members can still enjoy the original reading rooms, numerous lectures and even concerts.

Looking back at the history of the Lit & Phil's location takes us to Roman times. Part of the building stands on top of Hadrian's Wall, and a small part of brickwork can still be seen in the basement area. The Wall ran through Newcastle, joining at the Castle Keep, where it also doubled up as strong city defences.

From the 1100's to the 1500's Newcastle was a city at war as the Scottish constantly tried to conquer Newcastle and force the English back down south. During this time, the city walls were the main deterrent, with many deaths on either side of the Wall. The site of the building at the bottom of Westgate Road, also connects it to the West Road a well-known Roman road leading in and out of the City.

During Medieval times, the road led directly to the Blackgate and the Castle Keep. The locals would often line the street to watch the latest villain being led to the gallows or gaol. These would have included people accused of theft, to women being accused of being witches, which is well documented in Newcastle folklore. This leads us up to 1825 when the Society's members decided to build themselves a home in Bolbec Gardens which is now lovingly called The Lit&Phil.

GHOSTnortheast investigate 4 main areas of the library. Firstly the 1st floor which is filled from floor to ceiling with books dating back to when The Society began. You never forget the first time you walk into this room with it's beautiful domed glass ceiling. Breath-taking springs to mind.

During investigations, we commonly have EMF fluxes, shadows moving around the upper floor balcony and noises reported that sound like pages of a book being turned. I can recall walking into this area shouting out for the Teamleader and hearing a very clear "shush," which I thought at the time was the team involved in the investigation. It wasn't until I walked around the corner that I discovered I was the only one in there. It still sends a shiver down my spine.

Our Hub Manager David Howland experienced his scariest moment in the main library area. He described seeing a dark figure at the southern end of The Library that seemed to move forward towards him before leaning across a table. I verified seeing the figure as I stood next to him, and there were also several guests above us on the balcony who saw it too. David still cannot explain who or what was moving around the room that night!

The Loftus Room and the original Gents Toilets are another area where activity is rife. Many people have reported the feeling of being strangled in the Gents, whilst women feel extremely uncomfortable if left alone in the Loftus. A man's voice has been reported on numerous occasions by both guests and members of our own team. During callouts in this room, it is not unusual for us to experience both EMF fluxes and our K-2 meters bouncing up to the red marker. We have experienced banging and footsteps above us when we know there is no-one upstairs to create the noises. Is whoever or whatever still lingers in here trying to communicate and tell us their story?

Finally, is the basement, for us the most active of the locations within the Lit&Phil. Footsteps, shelving moving, female voices and moving shadows have all been reported. I would suggest visiting our YouTube channel to see some of the video footage we have caught there.

One of the most unusual pieces of footage is of a locked off camera that was left to record while we were taking a break. It is recording the empty corridor when you can hear the door to the right opening. This is followed by what sounds like footsteps walking past the camera.

Overall, as GHOSTnortheast's Lead Investigator, I must admit to The Lit&Phil being one of my favourite locations - whether I visit it during the day and see it in all its glory, or at night when it has a more sinister feel.

DIARIES OF THE INVESTIGATIONS.

INVESTIGATION #1.

When we were approached by partners at John Lewis Newcastle to see if we could help them to fundraise for their Charity of the Year, "Barnardo's," the GHOSTnortheast Team didn't hesitate to organise an investigation for them with all the money raised going to help the excellent children's charity. So, we gathered in the centre of Newcastle on an extremely warm Summer's evening to begin an overnight hunt of one of our favourite locations.

After the mandatory meet and greet we moved into The Lecture Room to start the group callout. During the callout, guests reported an unusual darkness in the far corner blocking their view of 2 of the guests. Temperature drops and draughts were felt around the group. We had earlier checked all windows and doors and concluded we could not locate the source of these draughts, although we could not rule out it being natural due to the age of the building.

I was leading the session and several guests say they witnessed a dark figure or shadowy shape following me as I conducted the callout. At the time I felt nothing of note during this time, however I felt quite dizzy just after the start but had put this down to tiredness. After the call out finished, the guests split into 2 groups to spend the rest of the night investigating the rest of the building.

The First Floor Library.

Group One conducted a Frank's Box session and reported several intelligent answers to their questions as movement was reported around the balcony areas. They then moved into the Committee Room. The room seemed quiet with little response until they came to leave. Both the K-2 Meter and EMF meter showed fluxes above the level measured during our baseline tests earlier in the night.

Group Two also reported that someone was above them on the balcony. They also heard footsteps coming from the same area. This led them to investigate the balcony where a guest reported being pushed when no-one else was near them. Later, when Group Two were using the Frank's Box, they asked if it could describe the building and the answer that came over the radio was "Books". The Frank's Box is a radio that has been altered so it constantly scans. Could this be merely a coincidence?

The Dowsing Rods were used in the bottom left hand corner of the upstairs location.
After a series of questions, the rods were moving and using yes and no answers we concluded that we had apparently contacted the spirit of a man that had died in the library but we didn't get any further confirmation of when or how.

The Loftus Room

Group One started with the Planchette experiment in The Loftus Room.
This started to move around and give answers that

were personal to one of the guests. (We do not share any personal message). The Planchette then started to move around in circles becoming faster and more violent until it finally came off the table with force. I asked one of the independent witnesses his thoughts, he answered "I'm gob smacked, I've never seen anything like it." I continued," Do you think it could have been pushed." He replied, "It couldn't be, it was going in so many different directions, I just can't explain it."

Group Two reported no response on the same experiment but witnesses saw a shadow walk between the bookcases, followed by EMF fluxes.

During both groups' investigations of the old Gentleman's toilets, they had several guests reporting a tightness around their necks and the feeling of being strangled. This has been reported in this location on many previous investigations. It is mostly reported by male guests to point where we have had guests leaving the area and returning to the Hub until they felt better. Another interesting occurrence that was reported in this area was flashing lights. The group thought that there was someone outside using their camera but on further investigation no-one was in this area. This was followed by a scratching noise.

The Basement
Both groups experienced activity in the Basement, although in different areas. In the shelving area Group Two started calling out down the corridor. All the guests could clearly hear the shelving moving and

footsteps in front of them. This coincided with Mandy, one of the Teamleaders, having to leave the area after feeling extremely angry for no apparent reason. I must say, it was the first time I've ever seen her leave a location.

Group One hadn't experienced much activity in the shelving area, so they moved on into the Boiler Room area. Here, they called out while using the Pendulum. This reacted to questions and the group found that there was a spirit that claimed to be afraid of men. The group also reported shadows moving in the bottom of the room, with the feeling of them moving around.

The Lit &Phil delivered some excellent activity on the night leaving us with as many questions as answers. Who or what had moved the Planchette? How did the shelving move? And why do men always feel like they are getting strangled in the Gents? Some of our guests couldn't explain what they had witnessed on the night leaving us with another night to sit and ponder about what we had witnessed. Overall, a good night of activity and the guests raised over £350 for Barnardo's!

Investigation #2:

We started the group call out in a different location for a change, using the Loftus Room. After a few false starts due to nervous guests, we got the callout underway. We had positioned an EMF meter and K-2 in the centre of the room. (Previous reads had indicated no electricity in the area). However, not long after calling out, the meters both started to respond to request. First, we asked for the lights of the K-2 to flash which they did on several occasions. We then asked for the EMF meter to be affected, again on several occasions we had high levels shown on the meter. The one thing that was unusual, on top of the responses, was that the meters never went off both at the same time.

Also, during the callout we recorded clear banging noises in the far-left side of the room where no-one was present. These raps were recorded responding to request. You can clearly hear me ask for whoever is present to bang 3 times, then the raps respond accordingly. I asked 5 times, and everytime the right number of raps are heard. After such an active session, we will be repeating our callout in this location at future events.

The Basement

The stacks in the Basement were as active as ever. Every group reported hearing bangs and taps throughout the area. Footsteps were reported and 3 separate guests reported feeling a presence behind them. One group reported a light at the bottom of the room that simply came and went. We tried to replicate the light with every natural cause possible but the group could not explain what this was.

This group also experimented with our laser pen that projects dots of light. All members reported witnessing some of the dots completely disappearing and then re-appearing on request, again something that we could not explain naturally.

Finally, in the Basement, a guest took quite an extraordinary photograph. As usual people were taking photos of the area, but on returning to the Hub one lady flicked through her photos to discover a very unusual light anomaly. We have no explanation whatsoever for this photograph.

The Loftus Room:

As the groups re-visited the Loftus Room all of them reported several unexplained noises very similar to the ones heard in the earlier callout. Also, a guest was reporting feeling very warm but on investigation with the thermometer she was 4 degrees cooler than any other person in the room. Also in this location, 8 witnesses reported an extremely loud banging on the door as if it had been slammed. Video footage proved that everyone was accounted for and no-one was in the area of the door at the time.

The First Floor Library:

The Frank's Box was used in this area with some interesting results. One group reported the box stopping on both German and French channels several times during their vigil. This has been reported several times before but The Lit & Phil seems to be only location we get this particular response. We still haven't established if it's because it is in the right place to receive these channels, or if it's something trying to get a message across.

Also on The Frank's Box a second group reported some direct answers to questions. They asked twice, "How many people are seated around the table?" On both occasions, you can clearly hear "9."
Indeed, there were 9 people sat at the table.

Also, on the balcony that runs around the library area we had reports of a figure walking around. The description of the figure was exactly what we have had reported on several previous investigations. Apart from members of the team, this figure is only ever seen by women.

The Lit & Phil delivered as usual. We had many reports of activity that seems to be repeated on a consistent basis within the same areas of the location. However, the photograph that was captured in the Basement by a guest is still fascinating. Is what was captured a natural occurrence that we still haven't explained? Or could it be what moves the shelving when everyone can hear its footsteps?

Investigation #3:

So, 2015 started with our annual fundraiser for The Literary and Philosophical Society or the building lovingly known as The Lit &Phil. It is the 4th year we have started our ghost hunting year raising money for this beautiful building and the night didn't disappoint. It started out in the Lecture Room with a group callout. Although it was a quiet start we did record irregularities on our K-2 Meter that we had placed on the floor of the room. Earlier reads had shown no movement on the meter at all. Then, as we called out, 3 guests had to leave at various points after feeling ill or dizziness. However, as soon as they left the room they all felt fine.

The First Floor Library/Committee Room:

While one group reported little activity in the main library area, they did report taps and a quiet banging noise in the Committee Room. In this room, everyone was seated around the table when the Teamleader asked for someone to open the doors. Within seconds both doors of the room flew open. It was a breezy night so we cannot rule out a draught causing this. However, the phenomenon did not happen again at any other point of the night. Was it merely a coincidence that they opened at the exact time as the request?

The second group was the other way around; they reported nothing in the Committee Room but witnessed activity in the main library. They stood on the balconies at the west side of the library, where they reported several bangs that they couldn't explain.

Loftus Room/Gent's Toilets:
There was little to report from this area from any of
our groups. One guest did report the feeling of being
strangled in the Gent's. (This is often reported and
has featured on previous investigations).

A noise was recorded in The Loftus Room which
resembled a chair being moved while no-one was
present. Unfortunately, we cannot verify if any chairs
had moved during this event.

The Basement:
Definitely the most active location of the night, with
both groups and a small group of team members
reporting activity in this area. Indeed, I witnessed
some extremely strange activity which left our
resident sceptic questioning what had happened. 4 of
the Team were at the bottom end of the shelving
when the top end of the room slowly lit up. We
genuinely thought that the caretaker at entered the
room with a torch. Our Hub Manager David then
decided to walk up to meet him, as we could clearly
hear movement. As David got to the top he stopped
dead in his tracks and turned towards us with a
puzzled look. "There is no-one here" he said with a
shrug. We joined him to find that the light covers we
had put on earlier had fallen off. Now, I can
guarantee the light cover was secured as I had
installed it earlier. Not only that, but what had been
moving around?

We replaced the cover securely with 3 witnesses to
confirm it could not just fall off or be blown off by a

draught etc. We returned to the bottom of the shelving and called out. Again, we could clearly hear movement, and again the end of the corridor lit up but not as bright as before. We all ran to the end of the corridor and again the cover had been moved but not removed as before. We viewed it back on the video, and this proved no-one had entered the room!

Our Hub Manager is also our resident sceptic, who simply shrugged his shoulders and said that he had no explanation at all to what he had witnessed.

As the investigation carried on one of the group of guests reported seeing something moving around at the top of the corridor but when they investigated nothing was there. They also reported seeing a strange light about halfway down the shelving corridor, that seemed to go bright then fade rapidly. We have examined the area extensively and cannot find a natural reason for this.

If the Basement hadn't delivered enough the next group was to witness another unexplained event.

Again, they called out in the shelving area. Both K-2 and EMF Meters fluctuated without reason before a bright light lit up the bottom end of the corridor for approximately 45 seconds. Again, on further examination not one of the guests or team could explain what we had witnessed.

Investigation #4:

After weeks of planning and 8 weeks after announcing the winners of our prize draw, the Birthday celebrations could begin. Everyone who attended had been to a ghost hunt in the past 5 years and the winners received 2 tickets for free to help the team celebrate this fantastic milestone.

We chose The Lit & Phil as our regulars will know it is probably the closest location we have, that we can call home. This is because it was our 3rd location and our first exclusive for public hunts, so it seemed fitting that we were here to have our "Birthday Party".

The night started with a huge thank you from the team which included every team member from the past 5 years apart from James Turnbull who unfortunately couldn't attend.

We then presented some facts and figures and how we have evolved in the past half of a decade.

We then moved on to the group callout in the Lecture Room. We had nothing of note to report although we did have a guest that had to leave after becoming upset as she felt that something was touching her. She did return after a short break.

The First Library/Committee Room:

The Committee Room became the centre of debate for this hunt as 2 of the groups witnessed the same thing. Both groups were sitting around the table calling out when the doors opened. Both groups told how they closed the doors and they remained shut until they called out and asked for the doors to be opened. The doors then opened on request.

We are aware that the doors can open when it is windy, however on the night there was no wind of note outside, and we had not recorded any major draughts caused by other doors being opened.

We tried other tests to see if there was a natural draught in the area but they all came back negative. Two guests were asked to hold the doors shut and both reported separately that it felt that something was tugging at the doors. The second witness said it took some force to keep the doors shut. A third group had reported that they definitely shut the doors behind them but when they got downstairs to the main library area the doors were wide open and none of the people present can recall hearing them open.

Was this just a natural draught? Although I must add that we have been investigating this location for nearly 5 years and the only other instance of this phenomenon occurred on 10 January. We haven't had any reports of this nature before this, even on stormy nights.

Also reported upstairs were several strange lights mainly around the balcony area at the back of the room. We did cover the windows to rule out any outside influence, but couldn't find an explanation.

The Loftus Room.

We reported nothing of note on the Planchette in this area. However, during one vigil, footsteps were reported coming from the back of the room followed by reports of shadows seeming to move in the same area. We had a guest reporting a feeling of anger and sadness in the area when the Teamleader was talking about the library. This has been reported many times in this area.

The Basement.

The Basement delivered again, with some strange goings on that have happened in this area on many of our previous investigations.

Footsteps were clearly heard walking towards the groups; shadows moving around; and the reports of the shelving moving from further up the corridor. Two groups reported hearing the door that connects to the boiler room area opening as if the handle was being moved, but no-one was present when they investigated further.

The pendulum was used in the area by separate groups and three of them all reported the same answers with movement of the pendulum. Using a series of controlled questions and movements with the pendulum, these groups all gave the same answers as far as getting the same initial to who was communicating with us.

Probably the best report in the basement was a group who reported hearing a voice, although they couldn't understand what was said. All 8 people in the group had heard it and described it as being a deep voice that seemed to whisper in a low, chesty tone.

Investigation #5:

We started the night with a group callout. Guests reported the room going unusually dark (remember, the room should really lighten up as your eyes adjust to light). Cold blasts were reported on people's legs in various parts of the room. However, although we can't rule out natural draughts, there was no wind at all on the night.

The First Floor Library/Committee Room:

We did receive some good reports of activity in the Committee Room. One group reported several flashing lights in the room with no natural explanation.

We called out with the Frank's Box and our new experiment with lettered dice. When the dice were randomly thrown the word, "Frankie" could be seen. At the same time, all the group reported hearing the word "Frankie" coming through the Frank's Box.

All three groups reported several taps and unexplained noises within the room. One group also recorded a series of flashing white lights within the room, as if there was lightning inside the building.

Also, upstairs we caught some unexplainable activity on video during our first LiveLink. A noise can be heard which sounds like a man sniffing followed by a couple of bangs. Straight after a light seems to glow

on the right-hand bookcase, before becoming very light. The light has a yellowy haze, and lasts 25 minutes before instantly switching off. We can verify no-one was in this area at the time and we have no explanation whatsoever for the light source. I have watched this clip back many times and still cannot find an explanation. Watch it for yourself on YouTube.
[https://www.youtube.com/user/Ghostnortheast].

Basement:
The Basement delivered yet again. During one call out the shelving could clearly be heard moving and shaking on request. At the same time, several guests reported seeing a shadow at the top of the corridor moving from side to side. Again, on further investigation, no-one was present in this area.

In the boiler area, we had good responses on the EMF which seemed to be communicating that we were talking to a soldier. This is consistent with earlier investigations where we seemed to contact a Roman soldier.

Overall, another night to remember at the Lit & Phil. Witnessing the same activity on numerous occasions fascinates me as an investigator. Then when you think you have seen everything a location offers, something completely different and unexpected happens. Tonight, hearing the same words on the radio that had just been rolled on the dice seconds earlier left me scratching my head!

Investigation #6:

Nestled in between the Castle Keep and Central Station in Newcastle's City Centre, this Victorian library still gives us goose bumps as we arrive. The team were looking forward to another night at one of GHOSTnortheast's favourite locations, as we were joined by a group of students studying Psychology.

We set up our LiveLink cameras in the exact same place as our previous investigation in the hope we would record the same level of activity as last time. We then started the night with our group callout in the Reading Room for a change to our usual Loftus Room. The callout started quietly with the only noises of note coming from the street outside. We then used the K-2 Meter near two guests who were reporting feeling cold. Although the thermometer reading didn't change they insisted that their legs were getting colder. As the callout continued, the K-2 started to fluctuate on request. Several taps were then reported around the room.

The Reading Room:

We conducted our Planchette experiment in this area. We did not get a response to our controlled questions, but two groups reported the Planchette repeatedly moving towards the same seat of the circle, although different people had taken turns to sit there. The EMF Meter showed several fluctuations with all three groups, and seemed to respond more when the men asked questions.

The First Floor Library/Committee Room:

The Committee Room is rapidly becoming a very active area of the Lit & Phil. All three groups reported similar activity during the investigation.

All the groups reported the doors opening to the room when no-one was present. We investigated natural causes, such as draughts, but could not find anything of note. Two of the groups reported the room seemingly to darken on callout. We did consider that we do sometimes get light pollution from the pub opposite but agreed that this should be making the room lighter not darker.

Two guests and I had problems with electricals here. One guest had a torch with brand new batteries, only for it to lose all power in this room. However, once he left, the torch immediately came back on. Was this just a faulty connection?

We had set up our LiveLink camera in the Main Library area, and as on our previous LiveLink our viewers seemed to witness something unexplainable. During the link, there were various noises recorded, many of which would have been quite normal. However, after only 20 minutes into the broadcast viewers reported that a female voice clearly says "Mummy". I have played this back many times using software to analyse the sound, and I can say we have no explanation to where this voice comes from. The recording is currently on our YouTube channel.

The Basement:

This area never fails to surprise the team. All three groups reported activity in the shelving area, with most reports repeating activity from previous investigations. The EMF has been known to fluctuate violently in this area, and tonight was no different. Two groups reported seeing a black figure moving at the bottom with every guest describing it as if it's someone popping their heads around the corner.

We also witnessed a light source at the far end of the corridor only to see it disappear as we got closer. Again, everyone described the area as feeling very disturbing, especially the females.

The Lit & Phil is certainly consistent. We seem to experience the exact same activity in the same places everytime. This time, the LiveLink recording left me scratching my head, as I have no idea where the noise came come from. Once again, The Lit & Phil leaves us with more questions than answers.

Investigation #7:

Our first visit to the Lit & Phil during the autumn/winter season was going be another very interesting night as the Lit & Phil seemed to want to share some of its secrets again. It was to prove a night of people wanting to leave and some extremely strange noises!

We started the night with the usual group callout in the Loftus Room. Within a few minutes one of the guests was asking to leave the room as she felt unwell, although she felt perfectly well before the callout.

The group reported that the room seemed extremely dark in places and we recorded minor taps and noises around the room. The guests then reported that they could see what looked like a dark figure following me around the room. Interestingly, halfway through the callout I had to leave. It's the first time in nearly six years I have had to leave a location as I felt light headed, dizzy, and as if I wasn't even in the room. I lost all orientation and couldn't decide which way I was facing. It was so intense, I needed help to leave the room. Ironically, as soon as I left the room I was perfectly alright.

The First Floor/Committee Room:

We conducted our Frank's Box experiment upstairs in the Committee Room. Although we did seem to get some clear words that were in response to the questions asked, we had nothing that matched up to our previous visits.

One response that was extremely interesting was when the question how many people are in the room was asked. The Box confirmed the right number. When asked to repeat the answer, the Box again broadcast the right answer.

Other reports in this area were that multiple guests were feeling extremely agitated, especially by the Box playing. This was felt by multiple guests in different groups, but it seemed to be concentrating on the female guests. Two of them had to leave the room after feeling very uncomfortable.

The Meeting Room:
We conducted the Planchette experiment in this room. Two out of the three groups both recorded movement on the Planchette with some clear words drawn out on the paper. I'm currently researching the content.

During one of the active Planchette sessions we recorded a voice on our camera. This was not heard by the group at the time, and we only discovered it on the playback. We think it says "Die." We have slowed the recording and filtered the sound, and it clearly seems like a human voice that was not heard in location. This video can be viewed on our Facebook page. Was it indeed the voice of ghost or a natural sound that we have mistaken?

The Basement:
It was business as usual in the Basement. As in

previous investigations, the groups all reported footsteps, bangs and taps in the area. One group reported clearly hearing a humming or singing of what seemed to be a woman's voice.

Another group had a very successful Dowsing Rods session. Using "yes" and "no" answers, the responses the group got did seem to confirm information that we have received in previous investigations. I can also confirm that the guests in this group had not been present at our previous nights in the Lit & Phil.

Another report by the groups was the constant changing of light levels in the corridor. It is another phenomenon that we seem to be reporting regularly in this location. The sessions start in total darkness but as we call out we get parts of the room that seem a lot lighter, before going dark on request. There is no natural light source in this area, as we are underground, therefore we are still looking for a natural explanation to this recurring phenomenon.

Investigation #8:

The Lit & Phil became our home for the 2015 Halloween investigation.

The Piano Room:
We conducted the group callout in this area. The night started slowly but soon picked up pace as people started reporting movement in the room. I was constantly asked where I was standing in the

room, as some guests were reporting seeing someone moving around the circle.

Temperature drops were reported in three areas of the room. What was unusual was the areas where the temperature dropped were nowhere near the windows or doors that could have caused natural changes.

We then split into our smaller groups to start the night. We conducted the Frank's Box and Black Scrying experiments in this area. Although we did get some responses on the Box, nothing seemed to be relevant to the building. However, one guest did say that she thought the answers did seem to make sense to her.

Several guests reported seeing changes in the Scrying Mirrors. A bearded man was reported on several occasions, by both men and women.

The Gentleman's Reading Room/Toilets:

Several guests reported feeling a sense of tightness around their necks in the toilet area. This has been reported lots of times in past investigations. One guest came out of the room and reported a burning sensation around his neck. On closer inspection, he had a bright red mark right around his neck. He said that he'd felt something tight around his neck then a sore, burning feeling. We checked and confirmed he was not wearing any jewellery, which we thought might have caused the sensations.

We also had many reports from the female guests of feeling very uneasy in the reading room. They were reporting shadow movement around the bookcases, with one guest saying she felt she was getting touched on the arm.

Again, these are similar reports to previous investigations that do seem to concentrate around the male guests in the toilet area, then changing to the females in the reading room.

The Basement:

We only use our equipment case and callouts in this area, as we always seem to report huge fluctuations on the EMF and noises in the book racking. Tonight was no different!

Two of the groups all reported seeing a figure move around the top end of the racking area, only to find no-one there when they investigated. There were also reports of footsteps, banging and what sounded like the racking being moved again. Interestingly, everyone in one group all reported hearing the boiler room door being opened and shut. As there is only one exit/entrance, no-one could explain who had moved the door.

The First Floor Library/Committee Room:

The best activity of the night in this area was recorded on our LiveLink video. This too can be viewed on our YouTube channel. As we were setting up the broadcast, we witnessed several noises that we cannot explain naturally. These were loud bangs right above our heads, and foot-steps walking on the balcony above us. Two people reported seeing a figure of a man in the far area walking towards the LiveLink zone, only to disappear as fast as it had appeared.

The noises that were heard seemed to continue through the night as the team moved away from the broadcast. It is now the second time I have witnessed a figure in the upstairs area of the Lit & Phil! Luckily, I could verify these experiences, because on both occasions someone else was with me.

Investigation #9:

The year started as usual at The Lit & Phil in the heart of Newcastle's City Centre. It was the annual fundraiser where GHOSTnortheast give all proceeds to Newcastle's oldest library, as it is still run as a charity.

We conducted the group callout in the usual piano room and it wasn't long before the activity started. During the callout, we had reports of temperature fluctuations, shadow movement around the room and light anomalies.

Several guests reported seeing a shadowy figure following me as I led the call out. I didn't feel anything unusual around me, but did feel disorientated on a couple of occasions.

During this callout, we also had three of our guests leaving the room. One had a fit of the giggles but couldn't explain why they were laughing. The other two reported feeling unwell and faint.

As soon as these people left the room they were

perfectly normal and couldn't give a reason to what had happened. This does replicate previous investigations, but we can't work out if it was just beginner's nerves or something more sinister.

The Basement:

In the basement, the smaller groups conducted various callouts and experimented with several of the tools to see what happened. All three groups reported hearing footsteps in the area when there was nobody in the room with them, noises from the shelving with two of the group further reporting movement of the roller racking.

One of the groups reported seeing a black figure at the end of the corridor, but no-one was present when they investigated further.

During a callout session in the basement we recorded something very unusual.

We record the basement at all times with our infra-red camcorders. We set it up so it is plugged into a mains socket and point it down the corridor towards the teams. A noise was heard by the team and when they approached the camera (as they thought that was the source of the noise) they discovered that the mains lead that connects into the back of the camera had been unplugged. We then watched the video footage before the camcorder lost power and it seems that the camcorder is pulled back before switching off.

We have nine independent witnesses that verified no-one was anywhere near the camcorder when it powered off.

Gentlemen's Library/Toilet:

We conducted the Planchette experiment in this area and we had answers to questions that have been received at previous investigations. We seem to have a name that has repeated itself now on five visits to the Lit & Phil. Research is still ongoing to see if it is linked to the building.

In the gentleman's toilet next door, we had two reports of guests feeling tightness around their necks as if they were being strangled. Again, this is a feeling that we have had reported several times in the past, and is always is focused in one particular part of the room.

Upstairs Main Library:

We used The Frank's Box in this area and during the investigation we recorded "Steven" eighteen times, all at different times throughout the night. Also in this area, guests reported seeing movement on the balcony in the main library. This was witnessed by six different people at the same time.

LiveLink:

It is worth looking at the LiveLink footage from this investigation. I was doing a live callout on the web, when the door to the room opened. I didn't catch the movement on camera, but the first time you can just hear the door open. However, a couple of minutes later I closed the door, only for it to reopen moments later. I still can't say if it was no more than a draught or if something or someone joined me in the room.

Another excellent night at the Lit & Phil, with the benefit that we raised nearly £500 for The Society.
Investigation #10:

Only 2 weeks after our first investigation of the year, we returned to Newcastle's oldest library as our friends from County Durham had decided to book their own private investigation of one of our favourite locations.

As everyone gathered for the night, a small concert in the building next door forced us to move our group callout from the regular Loftus Room to the Gentleman's Library area. This proved that sometimes trying something a little different can get you different results!

So, we gathered in the Gent's Library on the ground floor to start the night with a group callout. With all the shutters closed the room was exceptionally dark, especially the far end away from the windows. During the callout, we had two of our guests leave for the safety of the Hub as they started feeling disorientated and unwell. A few noises were heard around the room but we could not locate exactly what area of the room there were coming from.

The First Floor Library:
We investigated the bottom tables area for a time and used the lettered dice and Frank's Box. Twice, when asked how they died, the lettered dice spelled out the word "noose." This would usually just be noted for

later investigations but the same word was also recorded via the Frank's Box throughout the night.

The Basement:

As always with the basement, the location was to deliver as many questions as answers. All three groups reported footsteps in both the boiler room and the shelving area. These seemed to follow several EMF fluctuations in the area.

Two groups who were using the pendulum reported contacting a spirit and the answers they gave both linked to previous investigations and seemed to be connected to the Library. Several people all reported seeing movement at the bottom of the corridor. A photograph that was taken shows a dark mass here. We have filtered the photograph and can't explain what it is in the picture. We have ruled out natural shadows and faults on the camera. We have sent the photograph away for some more professional analysis and will report back what is found.

Investigation #11:

We started the night in The Loftus Room for our regular group call out. Within minutes we had a guest leave feeling nauseous and light headed. She was soon followed by two others during the call out. Ironically when we first walked into the room there were three chairs randomly in the centre of the floor that we had to move and I had jokingly said," I wonder if that means three people are going to go down?" Was this just a coincidence or something more sinister? There was very little else to report, so we split into our smaller groups to investigate the building

The Basement:

Footsteps were reported by everyone in the area. It seemed to be a mixture of sounds coming from above and in the room. The most intense came when footsteps were heard walking towards one of the group. These were witnessed by numerous guests, and the footsteps seemed to walk up and down on request.

A group had activity on the pendulum in the boiler room area that had links to information we have gained from previous investigations. This involves a young woman that is said to be linked to a time before the current Lit & Phil, when the land had a manor house built on it. A lady's voice was also reported twice in this area. It was described as a sobbing, although this cannot be verified as it doesn't appear on the recording.

Gent's Reading Room/ Gent's Toilets:

Two of our guests, from separate groups and with no connection to each other, both asked to leave the area. They were in the room calling out when they felt a tightness around their necks. One described it feeling like she was being strangled with something, the other said he felt like he was being hanged. This links into numerous past reports from this part of the building. Both guests were left shaken, and had to return to the Hub to calm down.

The First Floor Library:

Voices, banging and shadows moving around the balconies were just some of the reports in this area from all three groups. On our LiveLink we recorded a door to the Ladies' reading room open twice by itself. This is still on our YouTube Channel and follows some unusual fluctuations on both the EMF and K2 meters. Once again, this activity coincides with previous investigations. I must admit, the recording of the door opening on its own has kept many of the team glued to the screen, as we look for a natural explanation.

Investigation #12:

The usual group callout was relocated to the Gentleman's Library, as our usual location was set up for a fantastic display of local arts and crafts. The callout started slowly, with not a lot of activity to report. However, we then used the K-2 in the middle of the floor, which seemed to respond to questions. Just before we split into smaller groups, guests started to report movement behind them.

Loftus Room:

We conducted the Frank's Box experiment in this area, and one group received some very good results. When asked how many women were in the room, the group clearly heard "8". There were indeed 8 women present. We then asked how many men were in the room. The box answered "1". Once again, this was correct.

The name we recorded, and the answer to "how did you die" (from our baseline questions) matched what we have had numerous times before in this room. I'm not revealing these here, so we don't influence future investigations.

All three groups recorded Spanish speaking during their questioning. Again, this has been recorded several times before. Is this a coincidence? I must say I've lived in Newcastle all my life, and can't remember ever coming across a Spanish speaking radio station whilst searching for something to listen to. However, I do believe there is a link.

The First Floor Library:
All the groups reported activity in the main library area on the first floor, with movement around the balcony and the reports of a shadow figure walking around just two of the highlights. We also heard noises of books being moved and footsteps in the area.

One group reported hearing a young girls voice, but couldn't understand what was being said as it sounded very faint. This is the same area where we recorded a child's voice saying "Mummy". I wonder if this could be the same person?

The Basement:
The guests reported seeing a dark figure at the end of the bookshelves in the basement area. This is increasingly becoming the norm in this location. We have set up numerous cameras in the area and while we have had a couple of good photos (printed in our

magazine), we cannot seem to catch anything on video.

Two of the groups reported the shelving moving, and the door to the boiler room opening on its own. Then, in the Boiler Room, two groups seemed to have been in contact with a female, with both groups getting the same answers with the Pendulum. These were two separate groups, that were not connected and did not know each other.

Investigation #13:

We began the night in The Loftus Room for a group callout. The night started slowly but then guests reported movement in the room. Some of the group witnessed others disappearing into patches of darkness, with them describing the feeling of someone standing in front of them. Our experience is that this is usual activity in this room.

The room has a new glow in the dark clock on the wall. At first it was a bit of a distraction but then it proved to be the centre of attention. The group pointed out that the clock seemed to have a mist around it, which was blurring the numbers around the edge of the clock face. As we pushed this, it got more intense and the clock blurred more. This was witnessed by both GHOSTnortheast team members and some of our (independent) guests.

During the callout, the rooms' lighting also seemed to

shift. The room was going darker then lighter, but there was no light source in the room. We can't rule out natural eye adjustment, but in a dark room everyone would usually report the room becoming lighter and more focused as the eyes adjust. We have no explanation as to why it would vary so much.

Near the end of the callout we placed a K-2 in the middle of the room. We have successfully tried this before, and this time was no different. We placed it on a concrete floor away from any electric source. We always do pre-investigation base tests and found no activity in this area. However, during the callout, the K-2 was fluctuating from green to red on response. When we asked for whatever was in the room to go close to the box, the signal indeed strengthened sending the gauge to red; when we asked for it to move away, the gauge dropped to green. We did this several times to rule out coincidence.

We then split into our smaller groups to investigate the location hoping this was just the beginning of an active night.

The First Floor Library:
The Upstairs Library is a vast space, so the teams used the bottom end of the location. We had witnessed a lot of activity in this area in the past, and this is the quietest part of the room.

Two of the guests reported seeing numerous lights around the room. They also reported seeing a shadow like figure walking around the upper balcony area. One guest described it as someone who "was watching us to see what we were up to". Again, this has been reported on several previous visits.

Voices were also reported in this area. One group reported hearing what sounded like a baby crying in the area. This was at 12:30am and we are not in a residential area, so we can rule out natural causes. It does, however, link to YouTube footage we have, where you can clearly a baby crying and the word "Mummy" spoken aloud. Other noises included the sound of books been moved and pages being flipped. One guest commented to me that although the library was closed, it sounded busy? This has been reported before at a previous hunt, where a guest used almost identical words to describe the experience.

The Basement:

The Basement continues to stagger me with the constant reports of repeated events at every investigation. Reports tonight in the basement included footsteps, metallic sounds that suggested that the roller-rack shelving was being moved, and a noise that sounded like a lady singing.

One group was using the laser pen to light the corridor, and people reported seeing a dark figure at the far end, peering around the corner. This was in the same area that previous, unexplained, photographs have been taken. Who or what is this? I have tried every natural explanation that I can think of, but still have no answers.

4 THE LITTLE THEATRE
GATESHEAD

We only started investigating The Little Theatre in Gateshead in 2013 after being approached by one of The Theatre's Progressive Players.

There had been several reports of paranormal activity in The Theatre and they asked us to come and see if we could find anything. After our usual research and team only investigations we decided there were certainly some questions to be asked and opened the hunts to the public.

The actual Theatre has quite an extraordinary history. It sits on the edge of the well-known "Saltwell Park" in Gateshead and is spread across the purpose-built auditorium and two of the adjoining Victorian houses. It is believed to be the only theatre to be built during World War 2. The site was bought in 1939 with the generosity of two patrons, Ruth and Sylvia Dodds. The plot was once derelict but had been the site of

No.1 and No.2 Saltwell View. During the 4 years it took to build, it endured a string of War related problems. Firstly, in 1939 the building work had to be postponed due to the site being used by The Home Front using it to house a Barrage Balloon. Another setback came when all the windows and doors were damaged when a bomb fell onto the neighbouring Saltwell Park.

The Theatre finally opened in Oct 1943 and quickly bought No.3 Saltwell View to expand the building. Over the coming years, it thrived as it was home to "The Progressive Players Ltd."

Unfortunately, during the 60's and 70's everything had to go on hold as plans were drawn up for a new road and The Little Theatre was under threat to a compulsory purchase order.

Finally, the plans were withdrawn and in 1989 The Theatre bought No.4 Saltwell View and expanded further as it was now the only theatre in Gateshead. Due to a legacy left by a former member called Jim Ord and the fantastic work from The Theatre's volunteers, The Theatre has had a major facelift to the front, foyer and bar area. This was finished in October 2013 for the celebration of its 70th birthday.

Where do we investigate?
GHOSTnortheast investigate all three main parts of the theatre complex, including under the stage.

Auditorium and Under Stage Area:
I still remember on our very first visit to The Little

Theatre one of our Team Leaders screaming on the main stage as something made an extremely loud bang next to her. We captured this on video and it is currently on YouTube. We should have known then, that this little-known location in the world of the paranormal was to produce some unexplainable activity.

We always conduct our group callouts on the Main Stage and some of the regular reports from guests are footsteps around them and something dark following myself around the stage when I am the lead investigator. I never report feeling any different at the time.

Movement in the seating area is something else that is constantly reported with lights moving around without explanation.

We have had many guests leave this area after feeling unwell or not responding to the Team or their friends. This doesn't seem to be a specific group either as it happens to men and women.

Movement is often reported from the wings on either side of the Stage. There have been many reports of people thinking they have seen someone in this area, only to find no-one there on further inspection!

We also investigate under the Stage. There have been many reports of activity in this area with some captured on voice recorders. It is common to have reports of someone above on the stage. We have had footsteps reported and on 3 occasions people have reported hearing what they described as dancing above them. We have camcorders running at all times and they were played back to prove no-one was in the auditorium at the time.

EMF meters have seen fluctuations in this area, going from 0mg upto 10mg then dipping in response to voice. At the last investigation, a person was reported to be standing at the end of the corridor by 2 witnesses. It was only when someone went to get "The Guest" that it was discovered no-one was there and the corridor is a dead end (no pun intended). What did these people see? Was it a play on the light or a trick of the eye? After interviewing both people separately, I think they would tell you something different.

No.3 Saltwell View
This part of the location is the first of the terraced houses that were bought so The Theatre could expand and was built in the late 1800's.

We use the upstairs front room for our Planchette experiment and it has had some success. We have had the same shape and letters written on the paper on several different occasions with different groups and on different nights. Indeed, we have had what looks like initials written that would match up to the history of the house.

Also, on this floor is a changing room used by the actors and actresses. It seems a normal room, however many people have reported that this room feels very foreboding with many refusing to stay in there by themselves. We also have recorded what sounds like a woman's voice singing in the distance. This has been reported more than once in this room.

No.4 Saltwell View:

No.4 was the second house that was bought by The Theatre and is used as a rehearsal room and offices. Upstairs has also been converted for theatre use.

In the downstairs front room, we use our Ouija Board. This has had a mixed response. We have had direct answers to The Theatre and personal responses but nothing to indicate anyone linked to the house.

Our Dowsing Rods seem very responsive in this area with a lot of guests reporting movement to questions. Indeed, on many occasions when asked, "Where are you in the room?" the Rods always seem to point to the same place.

Upstairs, there have been many reports of footsteps heard on the stairs up to the attic room. We have investigated the small staircase but never reported any activity, however on returning downstairs, foot-steps are heard again.

On the corridor, there is a small room. Twice our Teamleaders have reported the room locked and asked for the key only to be told it is not locked and when they return the door is not only unlocked but open, leaving them completely confused.

Overall:

When I first researched The Little Theatre, I was not too hopeful as it was a relatively new building. However, how wrong could I be?

Researching the land where it stood and what was there before made me wonder what we would find.

Over the past 2 years it has led to some very active nights with even some of our more sceptical guests questioning what they had heard and seen.

I personally will not forget Natalie screaming on stage on the first night we investigated it or the look on our guests faces when they realised no-one was at the end of the corridor.

They say every good theatre has a ghost, well I think The Little Theatre has its fair share.

DIARIES OF THE INVESTIGATIONS.

Investigation #1:

Over the past 2 years The Theatre has become a firm favourite with both the team and guests.

After the meet and greet, everyone gathered on the main stage for the group callout.

During the callout, there were many reports of unusual activity both on stage and down in the seating area.

Several guests reported seeing something moving around the auditorium especially in the back rows of seats. Shadows were reported and a strange lighter area near the entrance doors. We quickly ruled out natural reasons such as light reflection, fire exit signs and light pollution from outside. The light seemed to fade then after a short time reappear.

On the stage, it really became peculiar. We had guests reporting sharp temperature drops beside them but the person standing right next to them couldn't feel it. This seemed to move around the circle. Footsteps were clearly heard and shadow movement seen at the left stage entrance. This has been reported several times on previous investigations. Guests also reported that it seemed I like was being followed around the stage by what they could only describe as a shadow, and they also thought I was waving my hands around in the air and pointing at people. Our video recording proves I was in fact stood perfectly still with my hands in my pockets, again this has been reported on previous events. As the callout was coming to an end two guests reported seeing a flashing light on the face of another guest opposite them. When I approached this guest she didn't respond to me at all. The person with her also spoke to her and again she didn't respond to our questions, so it was decided to remove her from the location. When she was outside the location she could not remember anybody speaking to her. Also what was strange was that myself and three other independent guests all thought she had not been wearing glasses when she had worn them throughout. We also thought she had her hair tied back but it hadn't been. Was this just a case of the lack of light playing tricks on our eyes or something paranormal?

No.4 House area:

We always have our Ouija Board in the old Victorian living room in the downstairs area. We did have some activity on the Board but most of the messages were of a personal nature and therefore we will not share the content.

Also in this area, there were numerous reports of a strong tobacco smell in the room. We obviously asked the guests if there were any smokers but the smell couldn't be singled out to anyone in the room. We also used Scrying Mirrors in the room with a mixed response. Two separate guests reported seeing an old lady in the mirrors and described her with "Dirty grey hair and wild eyes." This description came from 2 different groups at different times.

Noises were also reported to be coming from the adjoining staircase.

Changing Rooms/Upstairs:

In this area, we set up our Planchette experiment. Two of the groups did get movement with the pen but it was rather difficult to make out any letters or shapes that were drawn. However, we did get some good responses using yes and no questions. During one of the sessions we did manage to get answers related to a person and an event that we have had in a previous visit. I can confirm nobody in that group were present previously and we had not published our findings.

Other activity in this area led us to ask ourselves some serious questions. One group experienced knocking on a cupboard in the room. This seemed to respond to questioning, and even when they were asked in different ways the knocking responded the same. We checked the cupboard for anything that could have made this noise naturally but still have no answer to what caused this activity.

Also during a group call out at the table, we saw an object go shooting across the table. It turned out to be the back of a guest's earring. This may not seem strange or something actually quite natural, however the item didn't drop but flew forward onto the table. The guest in question reported feeling that something had flicked her ear. Our video footage shows no-one anywhere near the guest at the time and indeed the guest does not move in anyway until we hear the earring butterfly hit the table. We have tried several times to replicate how far the item travelled but could only get the same response by using force. We could not replicate it by simply dropping it out of the ear.

One group reported a shuffling sound coming from the Kitchen area. The first reported was ruled out as there was a member of the team in the kitchen at the time. However, it was reported twice more when there was no-one in the area as everyone was accounted for elsewhere in the building. One guest described the noise being like, "Someone wearing a large dress and it is dragging on the floor."
We have played back our voice recorders that were recording at the time but no sound is present.

The Main Stage/Basement:
All groups reported footsteps on the stage both when they were on the stage and below in the basement area. One guest recorded on his phone (which is on our Facebook Page) the sound that was described as someone dancing above.

We recorded the usual fluxes on our EMF Meters. The reads are taken before the night begins and in one area we have never recorded any electrical activity yet on investigation we get reads of between 3mg to 7mg which raise and fall during questioning.

Under the stage was to prove the most fascinating area of the night for one group in particular.

Whilst calling out as a small group noises and movement was heard at the far end of the corridor. One guest reported seeing a figure at the bottom which at first was dismissed by others as one of the team walking between locations. I went down to join the group and instantly asked for the guest at the end of the corridor to re-join the group to try a new experiment. The group fell silent as there was nobody at the end of the corridor. The earlier guest and I reported seeing the exact same person. The group again were convinced it was a member of the team walking around. It wasn't until they were led to the end of the corridor where the figure had been seen that they realised it was in fact a dead end (no pun intended).

It left the group quite dumbfounded as the only way in or out of this corridor would be to walk past the group. Did they see an apparition or was it a trick of the light? We will let you decide.

Conclusion:
It is not often I'm lost for words as a Lead Investigator, but being witness to firstly the knocking then to see what I can only describe as the figure of a person at the end of the corridor really left me without any explanation to an active night!

Investigation #2:

The night was clear and there was no wind to report. After the meet and greet we started the night in the main auditorium on stage for the group callout.

The callout started off relatively quietly but soon the

group were reporting movement in the seating area. Also reported was a strange shadow in the far-left corner that seemed to resemble a person sitting. The shadow did move on a couple of occasions but nothing was found on closer inspection.

Also reported was movement on the left-hand side of the stage behind the scenes. Several guests in that area reported hearing and seeing things in the holding wing of the stage but again nobody or nothing was found on closer inspection?

No.4 Saltwell View:

The Victorian house is used for our Ouija Board experiment. No group reported any activity of note on the board but all groups reported fluctuations on our EMF Meters. We also conducted 2 lone vigils in this area during the night with both "loners" reporting the exact same activity. Both reported that they were hearing footsteps moving around them and what is very interesting was they both pin pointed the footsteps in the exact same place.

Upstairs was quite interesting in that 2 groups reported that it seemed misty or smoky on the stairs. We checked for any source for this but we found nothing.

No.3 Saltwell View:

Dowsing Rods and EMFs seemed to be the tools of choice in this area. All groups reported activity when using this equipment in the old Victorian house. Names were reported and we are currently looking through our records to see if any match but none have appeared before at this location.

Noises were recorded in the upstairs front room around the sofa. Also, on the sofa the EMF Meter kept fluctuating on the same seat. I personally had taken reads before the investigation and can verify that it was a zero read in these tests.

Was something sitting on the sofa watching us? The Dowsing Rods seemed to move to a "yes" everytime we asked the question.

Auditorium/Under Stage:
Under the stage seemed to be the most active area of the night for all 3 groups.

All the groups reported hearing footsteps from above on the stage. As this activity, has been reported constantly on every previous investigation, we set up a camcorder recording this area. Both radio and camera checks revealed no-one on the stage when every group reported the sounds.

One group reported something being thrown in this area. The group was gathered at one end when something was clearly heard hitting the floor. It was a metallic sound like a coin. On investigation, a metal button was found in the area. We can't state that the button wasn't already on the floor but the group thought it was unusual that no-one had noticed it previously and they noted the coincidence that when thrown it made the exact same noise that they had heard.

Frank's Box was used on the stage with several responses recorded. Extreme temperature drops were reported in the area. Looking at the thermometer reads it did show drops of up to 7 degrees which only lasted seconds. We have checked for draughts in the area but couldn't find a natural reason for such changes.

Conclusion:

The Little Theatre always delivers a strange night. The noises recorded always seem to have no explanation. The corner of the eye movement leaves guests shaken up as they are often convinced they have seen something that simply isn't there when investigated.

Our database is filling up with similar reports in similar places but we are still struggling to find natural explanations.

Investigation #3:

The Team returned to Gateshead's Little Theatre on America's Day of Independence. Ironically last time we were there, a guest took a photograph that seemed to show the American Flag.

We hoped that Gateshead's beautiful community theatre that sits on the edge of the famous Saltwell Park would deliver the same levels of activity as in our past visits.

We started the night with a group callout on the main stage in the Auditorium. After a few false starts, with noises being ruled out as natural including a funny moment when a firework was heard outside making the group jump in fright, only to start laughing when we realised what the noise was.

We did start to get noises from above in the Gantry. A tapping was heard responding to the group, but what was unusual is that earlier before the guests had arrived, I had been up there conducting a pre-investigation callout.

We also had a guest who needed to be removed as she felt ill but the feeling disappeared as soon as she sat in the chairs below. A small group of guests also reported very cold draughts being felt, but we couldn't explain where the draughts were coming from. Both ourselves and our equipment had no answers to how these drops were happening.

No.4, Saltwell View:
We conducted our Ouija Board experiment in this area and apart from some minor movements, nothing was recorded on the board. Indeed, this location seemed very quiet all night with only a few fluctuations on the EMF/K2 meters.

No.3, Saltwell View:
We conducted our Planchette experiment in this area. Again, only one group reported anything of note on the Planchette which can be highly active in this area. The group that reported movement did receive some interesting information but with most of the information being of a personal nature, we will not

publish it.

Several taps and raps were reported by the groups, all seeming to originate from the cupboard on the near wall. This has been reported several times in past investigations. They do seem to respond to questions but are extremely faint and we are yet to find an explanation to what causes this phenomenon.

The Auditorium/Under Stage:

The Frank's Box did seem to deliver some very strange coincidences. Two of the groups both had the radio stop on wartime songs. Are these linked to the history of the land or a mere coincidence?

We also recorded a name twice that has been heard several times before in this location on different investigations. The name does link to the location but as soon as we start using the name the room seems to go totally inactive.

Under the stage, we had the exact activity that we report every time we are at the theatre!

Everyone is downstairs, yet the whole group hear clear footsteps above coming from the stage. It sounds as if someone is clearly walking right across it above. We have set up video recorder in this area, so we can play it back instantly to prove that there is no-one on the stage at the time.

We also recorded a lot of fluctuations on the EMF Meter in this area, although our pre-investigation measures so little to no movement in the same spot.

The Live Link:

I've included The LiveLink as it also delivered some highly unusual activity. We placed the Live cameras in a dressing room at the back of the building and during the start of the broadcast whilst I'm introducing the night you can see the lighting system flashing for no apparent reason. Also, you can hear footsteps outside the door, only for nothing to appear. We checked the times of these noises and can confirm that no-one was in the area at the time.

Investigation #4:

The Auditorium/Under Stage Area:

We started the night as always with the entire group taking part in a group callout.

It was long into the callout when the guests started to report some unusual activity.

At first several people reported seeing a figure standing in the far corner of the Auditorium. It seemed to move as we called out. The area was checked and no-one was there. There are only two entrances here, and no-one could have entered without being seen.

Also during the callout there were reports of major temperature drops on two parts of the stage. Using our thermometers, we recorded fluctuations of 10 degrees centigrade around a group of guests who had reported feeling exceptionally cold. We could not explain this and looked for natural explanations but to no avail.

Drops of 4 to 6 degrees were recorded on the opposite side of the stage again without any explanation.

After the group callout, the groups split into their smaller groups to investigate the building further.
When the groups were under the stage they reported hearing footsteps on the stage above. This is now a constant report in this location. We now record the stage area so people can look back instantly so they can see no-one is present in this area. It seems to range from a couple of footsteps to what sounds like dancing. We still don't have a natural explanation to what is causing these noises.

Noises were recorded under the stage area when we called out in loud voices, which was followed by the EMF Meter reacting to questions.

On the stage, we had the EMF seeming to match the groups voices. (We only seem get this activity in The Little Theatre and GHOSTscotland's Dunbar Townhouse).

We are currently researching why the meter only responds like this in these two locations.

No.4, Saltwell View:
We conducted The Ouija Board experiment in this area. One group seemed to get some interesting answers to their questions that coincided with the

history of the building.

We recorded some unusual noises in this part of location. Everyone who was present in the room reported hearing noises from above. It sounded like someone walking across the above room and then on the staircase.

We investigated the upstairs only to find the room above was locked. No-one was in the areas concerned, so we were left with no explanation of who had been on the stairs.

No.3 Saltwell View:

The groups took part in the Planchette experiment in this area of the location. Although we did get movement we didn't seem to get any information that was relevant to The Theatre.

One group did have an active yes/no session using the EMF meter.

Several knocks were recorded in the area by two different groups whilst the groups were calling out.
One guest who took part in a lone vigil in the laundry room at the back of Number Three had asked who had walked up to the door outside.

He was very confused when we confirmed no-one had been in the area whilst he was conducting the lone vigil.

Conclusion:

Yet another interesting night at The Little Theatre.

After many investigations of this location we are starting to see the same activity in the same parts of the location.

We are researching the location heavily to see if we can find natural reasons for the activity.

We've recorded the stage area constantly on several of the investigations and can confirm there is nobody on the stage when the groups are reporting hearing noises while they are underneath.

Investigation #5:

We started the night with a group callout on the stage in the main Auditorium.

We reported numerous knocks and bangs around us without being able to pinpoint the exact location. Shadows were reported in the seating area as well as behind the stage. A guest had to leave after feeling overcome with emotion, and she said this has never happened in the past.

No.3, Saltwell View:

We conducted the Ouija Board sessions in this area. There was some activity on the Board but a lot was of a personal nature (GHOSTnortheast never shares personal messages).

One group reported hearing footsteps on the staircase outside. We verified that everyone in the building was accounted for at the time and no-one was in that location. The group investigated the stairs both up and down but no-one was found. This has been reported several times in past investigations.

No.1, Saltwell View:

In the upstairs large front room, we decided to use the Planchette, however it was something quite different that scared one group and left them more than a little confused.

The group were near the Planchette when they heard someone walk past the room into the kitchen area. The group leader asked who it was and the whole group heard a voice say, "It's Marty." Marty is our Hub Assistant, so the group thought it was him. It wasn't until later when it was mentioned about Marty making a noise, that it came to light that Marty had been nowhere near the area. In fact, this could be verified by our LiveLink broadcast as he was present during the start of our YouTube program.

We checked with the rest of the group and again everybody was accounted for, so who had replied to the question and who had been making the noise in the kitchen?

Auditorium/Under the Stage:

Two of the groups reported hearing noises from above them when they were under the stage. This is one of the most reported occurrences at this location. It happens that regularly that we now have a camcorder set up on the stage to prove that no-one is around when this happens, it also has captured the sounds in past investigations.

The EMF on the stage proved to also confuse us on the night.

Its reads were constant until a group started to call out. The EMF kept rising up to its maximum levels on demand. At one point the guests said it seemed like it was singing.

The Team Leader radioed for me to see if I could come and find a natural explanation. After several attempts, I could find nothing that would cause of the fluctuations.

Investigation #6:

We gathered in The Main Auditorium for our group callout on the stage. It wasn't long before the guests started reporting activity in the area.

Firstly, people were reporting seeing shadows in the seating; this did seem to be moving within the seating area. This was followed by reports of temperature drops and freezing cold draughts in areas that had no natural causes.

The stage manager area on stage left seemed to be a hive of activity as people were reporting seeing some-one sitting in this area with several unexplained noises.

We had stood a young lady in a specific area of the circle as we often get the guests to participate. And as usual, the lady asked to move, saying she was too uncomfortable to carry on! Another guest then had to leave following an unexpected coughing bout, which mysteriously stopped when leaving the auditorium.

A third guest needed a seat and she needed water before moving on. The guests literally started to drop like flies and as we were on a stage that has a five foot drop at the front I felt it was too dangerous for the team and bought the group callout to an end. After the guests that had been affected had recovered, we split up into our three groups to investigate the building!!

No.4, Saltwell View:

We used The Ouija Board in this area however none of the groups reported much activity.

One group did report noises in the backroom area and when they investigated further, they found the door open. They said they definitely closed it earlier. The groups had also reported footsteps on the stairs and landing area. We also gained access to the attic area for the first time. Two of the groups reported shuffling noises in the attic and EMF fluctuations, however as it was a new part of the location, we had no baseline check details so cannot rule out this was normal.

No.3, Saltwell View:

In the main upstairs bedroom, we used our Planchette. We did receive a lot of yes and no answers to questions but we had nothing when we asked it to write or draw free hand.

A lot of movement and noises were reported in the corridors of the hallway upstairs but on further investigation nothing was found.

When we received the reports from all the teams at the end of the night, it became apparent that we had all had issues with our radios.

The Teamleaders all reported issues when trying to call out on their radios. We changed batteries but the issues were ongoing. All our equipment is checked before and after each night and we can't find an explanation to why the radios were not working on this particular investigation.

Auditorium:
The groups reported seeing movement throughout the auditorium and most of the activity was centred on the projection room. We had many guests seeing something moving around this area. The Projection Room is constantly locked on our nights and the windows are blacked out, so we can verify that no-one could have been in this area.

Under the stage, two groups reported the usual footsteps from the stage above when no-one was there. This has become such a usual occurrence that we now set up a video camera on the stage to prove no-one is there.

5 MARSDEN GROTTO
SOUTH SHIELDS

Situated at the foot of the cliffs that run from Sunderland to South Shields, The Grotto sits in the shadow of the famous Marsden Rock. This part of the North Sea was notorious for shipwrecks between the mouth of the Tyne and the Wear. There was many a ship fell afoul of the rocky coastline even up until the early 1940s, as they often came too close to land.

The history of the building is quite extraordinary and dates to 1782 when a local man, Jack Bates found a small cave and used explosives to create a larger cave for him and his wife Jessie to live in. This earned him the nickname of "Jack the Blaster."

Jack's new home was accessible by a series of zig-zag steps from the top of the cliffs, which it's believed he built himself. After word got around of the unusual dwelling, locals would visit the Bay and The Grotto to enjoy the beach and see the strange abode.

Jack and Jessie would supply refreshments to the beach users for a fee and probably created one of the first beach front cafes! It was also believed the Bay was used by smugglers and Jack was involved in the moonlight dealings of contraband. Jack died in 1792, ten years after creating his home. His family continued to live there until it fell into disrepair.

In 1826 a man called Peter Allan bought Marsden Grotto with money bequeathed by his father who had been a local gamekeeper. Immediately Peter restored The Grotto but also extended it to a 15-room mansion complete with ballroom and kitchen. He turned Jack's house into an inn and re-named the building The Tam O Shanter, changing it later to The Marsden Grotto.

The pub was an instant success with all walks of life, but especially smugglers and contraband runners. Stories are rife of smugglers tales including a smuggler being tortured and hanged where the stairs lead up to ground level. Legend has it, that on calm quiet nights you can hear the blood curdling screams of the young lad ringing around the cliffs.

The most famous story is of a young contraband runner in the mid 1840's who was befriended by an undercover excise officer. The officer used his friendship to find out all about the young man's work and one evening arrested him. A scuffle broke out and the contraband runner was shot dead on the beach below. Peter Allen, witnessing the whole event took the young man's tankard and emptied it on the floor, then proclaimed,

"Let no man drink from this tankard from this day forth, lest he be cursed."

He then nailed the tankard to the wall. Unfortunately, the tankard has been lost in recent times but a replica still hangs behind the bar. It's said on quiet nights the shots of the gun can be heard echoing across the beach.

Allan ran the inn with success, but became embroiled in a bitter legal battle in 1848.

A local businessman called John Clay bought The Leas and claimed that this gave him rights to The Grotto. Allan lost in court and was forced to pay £50 costs and £10 annual rent for the following 20 years! Allan sank into a deep depression eventually leading to his death only a year later. For the following 35 years Allan's family continued to run The Grotto.

Since then it has had numerous owners. The Harton Coal Company were proprietors in the late 1800's, allowing the building to fall into disrepair.

The local brewery Vaux stepped in and took over in 1898 and tried to clean up the area. They added the external buildings and later built the lift shaft as it stands today. In 1999, Vaux decided to close The Grotto down. It has changed hands several times since and was owned by Oxford Hotels and Inns whilst we investigated the building. It is now owned by a local chain of pub restaurants.

Paranormal Activity:

GHOSTnortheast have been investigating this unique location for nearly 5 years and we have had many reports of activity in various areas.

The Grotto Restaurant and Bar Area:

We have 2 areas that we investigate in the downstairs of The Grotto. Firstly, we have the Grotto restaurant area that sits behind the main bar.

We conduct most of our group callouts in this area and have had some success. We have recorded various bang, taps and clatters but we put most of these down to natural occurrences; However on one investigation we could clearly hear what sounded like barrels being dragged around from outside in the bar area. Also, we have had chains in the wall swinging to request. With the weight of the chains, we can rule out natural causes such as draughts.

Probably the most impressive response we have had in this area, is the footage we released on YouTube of a public investigation where we put a member of the group into the centre of the circle that we had created. You can clearly see the guests jacket moving to request. The guest involved was totally independent and said he didn't feel anything unusual but was very confused when he watched the footage back. We have been accused of using trickery to create the footage but the fact that we had 24 independent witness watching rules out any chance we would have to stage such an event.

We have also found the Planchette to be effective in

this area.

The Kitchen/Sitting Area:

In the other downstairs area, we have a sitting area near the kitchens. We always conduct our Frank's Box experiment here as over the past 5 years it has produced some excellent results. There is a well-known story of a small boy called Sam whose spirit is said to visit The Grotto. We have had the name Sam recorded on The Frank's Box over 50 times when asked. Coincidence?

We have also recorded several conversations in this area with the Box, particularly on one night where a string of 14 questions were answered consecutively with answers that made sense.

First Floor/Toilets/Mini Grotto:

An active Ouija Board and footsteps are regularly reported upstairs. On 14 occasions, we have recorded the same name on the board. These have been recorded on different night with different groups and different people. The Mini Grotto Bar area is also a location that seems to deliver strange results especially with female guests, with reports of shadowy figures, heavy breathing and a general feeling of being uncomfortable.

The upstairs ladies' toilet has been an area where there have been reports of unexplained lights (again, footage is available on YouTube) and there have been numerous reports of a figure seen near the mirror.

Overall, Marsden Grotto has a fantastic story attached

to it. Its unique position adds intrigue to its various rooms. I would recommend a visit whether you're popping down for a pint with your fish and chips during the daytime. Or when it becomes more foreboding after dusk when you can stand and look out to sea and imagine the skullduggery that took place many years ago.

DIARIES OF THE INVESTIGATIONS.

Investigation #1

GHOSTnortheast visited one of our favourite and most unusual locations for the first visit of the month before returning at Halloween.

It was a mild night on the North-East coast with very little wind.

We started the night with a group callout downstairs in the restaurant area located at the back of the bar area.

The callout started quiet with little activity to note until a guest started to report a cold draught coming across his head and face. Others then reported a notable drop in temperature.

First Floor & Mini Grotto
Two of the groups of guests reported footsteps coming from the mini grotto area. One guest reported hearing footsteps on the stairs up to the area from downstairs but when he looked nothing was there. Also in this area one of the groups reported seeing a figure move towards the stairs, again when they investigated further, there was no-one to be found.
During a dowsing rod experiment a group had movement to suggest that they had a female that was strangled and the name began with a M. This would not be so interesting until you have read what happens to a separate group in the downstairs restaurant area. To date, we cannot trace any history

of this name or any associated occurrence.

Finally, in this area, one of the groups reported hearing a large bang above them. There is nothing above this area except the roof which is flat. Usually we would put this down as some form of natural occurrence however, at the same time as they reported the noise, a member of the public was outside with one of the team. They reported hearing a woman's voice followed by a large bang. This was so distinctive from both sets of people that it led us to climb the outside steps to look on roof in case someone was up there. We found nothing.

Downstairs Alcove & Kitchens

We always conduct our Frank's Box equipment in the alcove area as over the past 4 years we have had some very good results.

Again, all 3 groups of different people and at different times of the night reported 2 names that were
the same. These 2 names constantly come across the Franks Box at this location. 3 other points of note were recorded but we are currently researching what was heard.

The most impressive sound clip was when a group of guests all heard, clearly, "Did you enjoy your meal?" The group all laughed as they had all enjoyed a meal in the bar before the investigation.

This group also experienced the table banging in front of them. "It seemed to lift into the air!" Was the exact quote. We tried to replicate the movement but couldn't.

Grotto Bar & Restaurant:

This area was relatively quiet with one exception. During a dowsing rod experiment the rods indicated that we had a female, who had been strangled and her name began with the letter M. This was a totally different group of people that had reported this upstairs.

Conclusion:

We have been investigating The Grotto for over 4 years and we seem to experience the same activity everytime. We get the same names in the same places but with different people investigating.

The Dowsing Rod experiment was quite extraordinary in the fact that 2 totally separate groups of people reported the exact same finding. At this moment in time I cannot verify any of the information given but still cannot explain it.

Was it a spirit returning to tell their story or a simple coincidence?

Investigation#2:

What a fantastic way to spend Halloween, surrounded by the history of Marsden Grotto. We gathered in the Grotto area to start the night with a group callout with a difference, using the traditions of All Hallows Eve and Jack O'Lanterns.

The callout started off relatively quiet but then a strange occurrence happened. On several occasions, the whole group witnessed a flashing light in the bottom of the room towards the original wood door of The Grotto. It was like a flash off a camera, so we sent someone outside to watch for any natural causes. The light happened again twice and both times no natural cause was found.

Alcove Area:
We conducted our Frank's Box experiment in this area. A few names were mentioned that we have heard before on previous visits. What was worth mentioning was all 3 groups recorded mentions of the devil. This could have been coincidence as it was Halloween!

Also in this area, we had female guests from 2 separate groups complaining about pains in their eyes and head.

Main Grotto Area:
The Planchette seemed to work for the groups but delivered personal messages. (GHOSTnortheast will not publish any personal information).

One group used a laser pen with some success as some of the guests reported seeing the dots of light seemingly disappear and re-appear on request.

Upstairs/Mini-Grotto:
Again, we recorded activity on the Ouija-Board but it was of a personal nature.

Two of the groups reported hearing banging coming from the north end of the restaurant. They also reported hearing footsteps and on further investigation no-one was found in the area.

As the groups moved into the Mini Grotto area, all three reported fluxes to their EMF Meters but nothing on the K-2s at the same time.

Several female guests reported feeling uncomfortable in this area, which again coincides with previous visits.

Lone Vigil:

A couple of guests braved the Lone Vigil. One gentleman reported seeing a small figure which he thought was a small girl in the area we put him in. He described it quite vividly and when we watched the video recording back there is an orb in the area in question. However, with all orbs we cannot rule out natural causes such as dust etc.

This has been reported before on the lone vigils but the gentleman has never been to The Grotto before. Overall a memorable Halloween.

Investigation #3:

On a bitterly cold but clear winter's night we visited Marsden Grotto in South Shields.

Unfortunately, we had been notified that The Grotto was now up for sale and this could possibly could be the last ever ghost hunt in this fantastic and unique location.

The Grotto, like The Lit & Phil had been one of our stalwarts for the past 5 years and regularly left us scratching our heads at the end of the night. This location seemed to deliver on our main experiments such as the Ouija Board and especially the Frank's Box. Tonight, was going to be no different.

We started the night with a callout in the cave restaurant area at the back of the building. 2 of the guests had to leave due to sickness and, this was to be followed by some quite extraordinary activity.

Some of the guests at the bottom of the room screamed and shouted as something metallic hit the floor. Initially I thought it was a stone had fallen from the ceiling but on further investigation it was a 10p piece. The man in the group reported something had hit his shoulder/head area then he heard something land on the floor. The lady next to him then reported that she'd had a 10p and a 50p in her pocket before the night started which was confirmed by others present with her. The 10p coin was now missing. The guests either side of her confirmed that she had not broken the circle and had both hands held by independent guests, ruling out the possibility that she could have thrown it her-self. Interestingly, she reported at the end of the night that her 50p coin had also disappeared.

Upstairs:
Several personal messages were received on the Ouija Board and reports of footsteps coming from the small grotto area. Also, footsteps of what was described as a child or small person were reported by 2 different groups whilst lone vigils were taking place in the upstairs ladies toilet. This has been reported on numerous occasions.

Cave Restaurant:

Again, the Planchette seem to deliver personal messages to some of our guests. A flashing light was reported again in this area and despite further investigations, we cannot explain where this light originated from. It is often described as like a camera flash, but longer.

Kitchen Alcove:

We conducted the Frank's Box experiment in this location and what followed was probably the best response I have witnessed!

The following transcript was taken over 4 hours and with 3 different groups and it seemed to centre around myself. This is not the first time………

G1- Do you have a message?

FB– Get Steve.

G1– Why Steve?

FB-I love you.

G1– Who do you love?

FB-Steve

When I arrived, the box went quiet. We would usually report this as coincidence until Group 2!

G2-Can you tell me your name?

FB– Man's name clearly heard but removed by us

G2-Is your name (Name Heard)

FB-Yes

G2-Do you have a message?

FB-Talk…. Steve

G2-Do you want Steve here?

FB-Quickly.

I came to the table…

SW-What's your name?

FB-Richard

SW-What do you want with me?

FB-Love

SW– Thank you, can you tell me how many people you can see?

FB-10 (Indeed there were 10 people around the table)

SW– I have to go but I'll return, will you stop the box on a love song?

Again, this could still have been a coincidence... but then came Group 3!

G3– If anyone is with us can you speak please?

FB-Steve

G3-Do you want to talk to Steve?

FB-Please

As I came to the table as he sat down the box stopped on The Hozier's track Take me to the Church.

SW– I asked for a love song thank you. Can you give me your age please?

The box went quiet after.

Conclusion:

I don't have an explanation for what happened on the box or with the coins. I can only say it was witnessed by different people during the investigation and is probably the best response we have had. Was it a spirit that had a crush on me or mere coincidence? We will let you decide!

6 THE CASTLE KEEP
NEWCASTLE-UPON-TYNE

Sitting proudly on the banks of The Tyne, overlooking the world famous Tyne Bridge is the building that gives Newcastle its name.

The Castle Keep is probably one of the finest examples of Norman castle building still standing in Britain. The Castle dates to 1172. But before we look at its industrious history we researched the land that it stands on.

A settlement on the site dates back as far as the 2nd Century when the Romans built on the land to defend their newly built Tyne Bridge which wouldn't have been as grand as what stands now. The Romans named the area Pons Aelius and it was an important asset to Emperor Hadrian.

During Anglo-Saxon times, the area became known as Monkchester and The Garth area became a burial ground.

In 1080, William I commissioned a wooden motte and bailey castle to be built. It was replaced by Henry II in 1172 who employed The Grand Mason Maurice to build the stone building that remains today. The additional 4 stone towers that corner the original Keep were added in the 13th century for added protection.

Due to the addition of strong city walls over the following years The Keep fell into disrepair with it being described as "ruinous" in 1589.

In 1643, the then Mayor, Sir John Marley repaired The Keep and brought it back to its former glory due to the ongoing English Civil War. A year later in 1644, The Keep enjoyed its biggest claim to fame as the Scottish besieged Newcastle. It took them 3 long months to finally crack the spirit of the Geordies and take the City including The Keep.

After the border wars ended, The Keep was used as a prison. Criminals ranging from pickpockets to murderers were thrown into The Keep to live in squalor. The building had no roof so the rain would fall into the Garrison on the ground floor where the prisoners were kept lying in their own mess. The conditions were horrendous. This continued into the 18th Century when prison guards would charge the public to walk around the prison like a freak show, humiliating the prisoners further.

In 1809, The Newcastle Corporation bought The

Castle and its surrounding Garth. Over the next 50 years it repaired the building and returned its roof.

The Castle Keep is now owned by Newcastle City Council and is still stands proud overlooking the Tyne and all of her bridges.

Where we investigate:
The Keep is quite a large location with its many floors linked by over 100 stairs. Many of our guests enjoy the long trek up to the rooftop before an investigation to enjoy the night time views.
However, we will start from bottom to top.

Ground Floor - Garrison/Chapel:
The Ground Floor is split into two main areas. First the Garrison which was used as the main prison in the 1800's. In this area, we have witnessed many strange occurrences including a shadowy figure standing in the main doorway. This has been seen on many occasions but seems to disappear when invited into the room. A story involving a little boy is common knowledge, but we have yet to encounter any evidence to back up this story. Temperature drops are often reported in the corner of this room with no explanation. EMF and K-2 Meters are often very active but we always need to examine the train patterns as their proximity can cause natural fluxes.

The second part of the ground floor is the Chapel.

We have had many reports of movement around this room. Also, we have had multiple reports of guests feeling like they are getting pushed when calling out.

We have witnessed sounds that were described as a chanting or singing. But probably the most intriguing activity we seem to get on a regular basis is a darkness. We have witnessed this on many occasions where the room has gone unexplainably dark around certain people. The room has windows that lets in some natural light but this seems to darken when we call out in a group. Indeed, recently I was taking part in a small group callout when it became extremely dark around one guest, to the point where we couldn't make out any facial features although we were only a few feet away. Is this paranormal or merely the light playing tricks with our eyes?

First Floor - Reception/Queens' Chamber:
We always conduct our Frank's Box experiment in the reception room. Over the years, we have had quite a few names that are linked with The Castle and strangely the Box seems to stop it scanning process on a regular basis in this location. The Box has also stopped randomly on radio stations broadcasting French. Footsteps walking around the edge of this room are often reported too.

The Queens Chamber is a small foreboding room. Not many of our guests will venture in by themselves as they often report a feeling of being watched or intimidation in there. We have witnessed a lot of temperature changes in this room along with some success on our Dowsing Rods. We have used beam breakers in this area and several times the alarm has gone off without anyone being in the room.

Second Floor - The Main Hall

On the second floor, there are several smaller rooms all running from the Main Hall. We always try and do our large group callout in this area and we have had some common results. It's reported almost like clockwork that someone is seen in the doorway to the stairs, noises that seem to be metallic and movement on the stairs leading from the main door.

But probably the most important activity of The Castle Keep has been witnessed in this room twice!

Firstly, one of our team was lying in the hall whilst on a lone vigil. On her return, she asked why no-one spoke to her when they walked past. When we explained that the entire team were elsewhere in the castle she looked quite shocked. She described seeing a pair of legs wearing dark boots walking behind her. She said she couldn't see further than waist height due to the way she was lying down. We still haven't been able to explain who she saw that night.

The second sighting was seen at the start of this year and was witnessed by an entire group of guests. They were using the Ouija Board (that wasn't very active) when they all witnessed a dark tall shadow walk across the bottom of the room. Again, we have no explanation of who was in this room at the time.

Overall:

The Castle Keep remains our oldest location with nearly 1000 years of history within its four walls and that doesn't include the history of the land it's built on.

Over the years and our many investigations, we have had many reports of the same happenings. The fact that we have had 2 reports of apparitions in the same area leaves us as GHOSTnortheast feeling that it is one of our most important locations.

DIARIES OF THE INVESTIGATIONS.

Investigation #1:

We travelled to heart of Newcastle's city centre for our next investigation of the month. The Castle Keep is a foreboding building set back from the lively club scene and sits proudly on the banks of the Tyne.

It was a warm night with cloudy skies.

We started with the group call out in the Main Hall. The guests reported numerous light anomalies including a shadow of a figure in the doorway to the stair well and a tall large dark figure on the stairs, looking into the Main Hall. Guests also reported hearing a metallic sound coming from the connecting Well Room.

Ground Floor-Garrison & Chapel:
Not a lot of activity was recorded in this location, however two of the groups separately reported extreme darkness around certain members of the group. Indeed, I witnessed a guest in the Chapel area who seemed to be surrounded in shadow to the point of not being able to make out his facial features from a distance; This was confirmed by other independent witnesses.

First Floor - Entrance & Queen's Chamber
One group reported hearing footsteps moving around the room, but were unable to pinpoint where they were coming from. Two of groups recorded strong

responses on the dowsing rods that after questioning both seemed to be talking to a young male.

A lot of EMF activity was also recorded but we are first trying to confirm train times as this can influence the meter due to the close proximity to the lines from the Central Station; (although after 12:30am there doesn't seem to have been a train out of Newcastle?)

Second Floor The Great Hall & King's Chamber:
This area seemed to produce the most activity on the night with all three groups seeming to encounter some form of activity.

Group One reported feeling extremely uncomfortable in the King's Chamber and all members of the group reported seeing a shadow like figure in the bottom of the room that seemed to move towards them when they called out. One guest felt extremely uncomfortable as it felt like "Something was in my face!" The same group reported that the room seemed to go from dark to light then back to dark.
During a lone vigil, a guest reported seeing white lights flashing above the archways and extreme feelings of cold.

Group Two seemed to feel similar experiences in this area and recorded that they heard numerous taps from the Well Room, like the group callout.

Two guests from Group Three were above the Great Hall on the balconies, when they reported seeing a figure move across the Hall and into the Well Room. We investigated further and can confirm no-one was in this area. We can confirm this is the third time a group have reported the exact same thing in this area all on different nights. Could it be the shadows playing tricks on their eyes and is it a coincidence that we have had this exact same phenomenon reported on three different occasion by three separate groups? As always, we will let you decide.

Conclusion:
Another good night in the centre of The Toon.

The Castle Keep has so much history it doesn't surprise me that we do seem to get many reports of phenomena but we as a group must be careful whilst doing our reports as the building is extremely close to train lines that can affect the EMF and K-2 meters. Also, it is close to various pubs and clubs, so sound pollution can have an impact. But even with these factors considered, we are left with some very interesting results!

Investigation #2:

This was the first of our visits to The Keep in 6 days as we would return the following Friday.

The night started with a group callout in the Great Hall. We had several noises reported from the adjoining Well Room that sounded like footsteps.
The group also reported several strange lights. A red light was reported, and while initially I thought it was the natural glow of the infra-red lamp on our

camcorder, the guests reported it to be more of a circle and it that was at chest height away from where the camera was located.

Shadow movement was reported on the stairway at the back of the room where there were reports of cold and one guest reported that they felt as if they were being touched on the shoulders.

The Garrison/Chapel:

Only one group reported any activity of note in the Garrison area. They reported seeing something in the doorway to the staircase. When I asked them to describe what they had seen, they said the only way to describe it was something dark that kept moving in and out. We have looked back at our video footage but nothing was recorded.

The Chapel seemed to deliver a little more. All groups reported EMF and K-2 activity but we need to be very careful as the location is extremely close to the train lines. However, one group did seem to get the field to strengthen and then fade on request which we captured on video.

Entrance Room/Queen's Chamber:

A recurring phenomenon in this area is the sound of footsteps in the entrance room that cannot be pinpointed to one place. All 3 groups reported this and although we had ruled out natural reasons such as noise pollution from above or indeed sound travelling from other areas we still can't give a reason to what caused these noises.

We also conducted a Frank's Box session in the area with limited response. We did have names and places mentioned but we can't say whether this is mere coincidence or indeed paranormal activity.

The Queen's Chamber was unusual. Reports of unnatural darkness and several guests reported movement in the area but on further investigation no-one was found.

The Great Hall/King's Chamber:

Again, movement was reported on the stairs of the Great Hall. We now set up a camcorder to monitor this area throughout the night as we get constant reports of activity in this area.

One group reported movement on the Ouija Board however as it was of a personal nature we will not report what was said.

2 groups reported fluxes on the K-2 that seemed to respond to questions; This was strange as it seemed to only light up to specific questions about the castle. I have checked on train timetables and I'm unaware of any trains being near the castle at the time of this activity.

We also had reports of guests being touched and pushed in the King's Chamber with a feeling of being watched.

The balconies above the Great Hall were active. I myself had earlier reported seeing what looked like a figure leaning over but when I went upstairs there was no-one around. This was confirmed by 2 other independent guests who seemed to see the same thing in the same area.

One group reported movement on the stairs when they were in the balconies. They thought someone had come up to join their session only to be left waiting for someone to appear. We confirmed the locations of the team to rule us out and we were all busy with our teams.

Conclusions:

Not as active as The Castle Keep has been in the past. However, the amount of movement that was reported in some areas leaves us guessing whether it was simply a trick of the moonlight or car headlights coming into the building or was there someone from the past walking around the Castle?

The footsteps in the hub area keep us perplexed due to the constant reports of this on not just tonight's investigation but on various previous investigations. Are we missing something natural that makes this noise or indeed are we hearing the footsteps of days gone by?

The Keep seems to deliver the same activity everytime we investigate it.

Investigation #3:

The Great Hall:/King's Chamber

We started our night with a group callout in the Main Hall.

During the callout people were reporting temperature drops in various parts of the room. We must consider that this is an old building and therefore cannot rule out natural draughts, however on our thermometers these fluctuations were quite extreme and lasted minutes rather than the seconds that would be expected from draughts.

Five guests all reported seeing a figure in one of the archways which leads to the stairways. On further investigation, no-one was found in this area.

We split into smaller groups to continue the investigation.

Activity was reported in The King's Chamber where we conducted the Ouija Board. Very little was reported on the board, however one group reported seeing a black figure beside the door that leads to the Great Hall; Minutes after this being spotted several of the guests reported sensations that felt like someone was blowing on them.

Whistles were also reported in this area but we cannot rule out sound pollution from the various bars nearby (although twice the whistle seemed to respond on request.)

1st Floor/Queen's Chamber:
We had numerous reports of people feeling very uneasy in The Queen's Chamber to the extent that one gentleman had to leave the room and sit out for a while as he reported feeling very queasy and thought he was going to be sick. Looking at the guest he had become very pale, although his colour returned when we removed him from the area.

The EMF Meters seemed to respond to questions in this area and confirmed responses that we have received on previous investigations.

We also conducted the Frank's Box in this area and again the radio constantly stopped on foreign radio stations. Since this visit I have revisited the Castle with a normal radio and scanning the channels, and I have only tuned into one French channel.

The Garrison/Chapel:
During the call out of one group, two guests reported smelling flowers in the Garrison. This of course is a famous story connected to the Castle, however we haven't had many reports of this in the past. Did the infamous Flower lady decide to visit us?

Whilst in the Chapel, one group reported some strange activity that directly links to some of our previous investigations, particularly a team only investigation we had last year and the information was never made public.

The group were calling out with little response when I

asked everyone with a hood to put it up. Instantly, the EMF Meters started to get louder and constant. The guests reported the rooms atmosphere had changed and some had begun feeling uneasy. One gentleman reported feeling as if his arms where being lifted into the air by themselves. I can confirm when the team conducted a similar experiment last year one of us reported the exact same feeling accompanied with some heavy EMF fluctuations. Was this mere coincidence?

LiveLink:

Our LiveLink camera seemed to cause some controversy with our viewers. Many reported seeing various light changes and a light figure at the top of the stairwell. But some also reported seeing a sandbag we had placed as trigger object move on its own. The group has been split, as some think it was the lighting system change that causing the shadows in the corridor to change creating what looked like movement. The others were convinced it physically moved. Watch it on YouTube and you decide for yourself.

Investigation #4:

For our penultimate investigation of 2015, we were heading to Newcastle's City Centre to return to The City's oldest building. The Castle Keep.

We warned our guests beforehand to be prepared for a cold night but it turned out to be quite mild inside the ancient building which made investigating it a lot more comfortable.

We gathered in the Great Hall to start the night with a group callout.

Immediately people were reporting shadow movements around the room. We also reported several taps and noises. However, we can't rule out noise pollution as we were in the centre of the city.

After a few minutes, we did record a very loud bang on the large door. It was loud enough to make some of guests jump. We investigated further to find no-one near the doors in question. As we carried on there were several reports of people being touched and a lot of reports about temperature fluctuations. Later we examined our temperature logger and it showed no natural changes to the temperature in the room.

The Garrison/Chapel Area:
It was quiet downstairs for two of the groups. However, one group was to experience something that he had been reported several times several years ago.

We were pairing up as the guests visited the Condemned Man's Cell to do a short call out. We keep the numbers small in this room as it is very small.

One female guest let out quite a scream and shouted for me. I immediately went and removed her from the room and as she calmed down, she explained that she felt something grab her just above the waist.

She looked at where she had felt the hand and she revealed a scratch across her back. The scratch was definitely new, as it had started to raise the skin.

This is not the first time we have had people scratched in this room. Indeed, about three years ago, I myself experienced a similar feeling and when I removed my top I had 3 large scratches across my back that ran perfectly parallel with each other.

Were these scratches made unconsciously naturally, or does someone in that room not like being disturbed?

Another strange report in the Garrison area was reports of a figure on top of the stairs. People initially thought it was part of their group as it was seen by a few of the guests at the same time. It wasn't until it seemed to disappear when questioned that they realised that the figure didn't belong to the group.

Main Entrance/Queen's Chamber:
We used the Frank's Box in this area. We did record several words and phrases but nothing of note that could be linked with either the questions asked or the building.

The pendulum, which is usually quite active in the Castle Keep, didn't seem to work on the night.
Again, footsteps were reported in the hub area whilst the groups were in The Queen's Chamber. This seems to be regular activity now within this location.
As the train lines were relatively busy upto 12:30am, we ruled out any fluctuations to the EMF and K-2 Meters in this area.

The Main Hall/ King's Chamber:

There was very little to report on the Ouija Board at this investigation. A couple of small movements but nothing that could be deemed as paranormal.

Several guests reported feeling very uneasy in The King's Chamber, although none of them could "put their fingers on it". It was quite unusual that all of them used that exact turn of phrase to describe the feelings that they were getting in this specific part of the location.

Voices were reported in the Well Room. We did explain we were near a walkway that it is used for revelers walking between The Diamond Strip and The Quayside but the guests that reported these voices were convinced the voices had come from inside the room and not from outside the building.

Conclusion:

A quieter night than usual for The Keep. However, the return of "The Scratcher" leaves us intrigued!

Investigation #5:

We have been investigating The Keep for over five years now and it always throws up new questions and new experiences and tonight was not going to be any different.

We started our group callout up in the Main Hall as usual.

The callout was quiet for most of the time. However, the group of guests at the top of the hall near the stairwell kept reporting noises behind them. When we called out for whoever it is was to come forward and join us there were reports of movement in the area.

The Garrison/ Chapel:

One group recorded a very unusual noise while in the Chapel. They described it as feeling a noise rather than hearing it.

It was a deep humming noise that did seem to reverberate around the smaller alcove. This coincided with our EMF recording several fluctuations although I'm am currently researching the train routes on that night so I can rule out any natural causes.

Ground Floor/ Queen's Chamber:

The groups used the Frank's Box in this area. We have logged the answers on our spreadsheet but nothing of note stands out from the answers except for both French and Spanish coming through.

Does this tie into The Keep's history or is it a mere coincidence?

Movement was reported in The Queen's Chamber at the back of the exhibition area. On call out several guests reported the temperature changing and said they had felt as if they were being watched but our equipment didn't record anything.

Conclusion:

The Keep has such a history and we always seem to

find something new on every visit. It seems to be a building filled with stories.

Investigation #6:

The night started in the Great Hall for our group callout.

It was a slow start with very little activity after we filtered out the motorbikes and drunken revelers outside. However, guests were starting to report seeing shadows moving upstairs in the Cloisters above.

At first, we had ruled it out as lights from outside traffic, but on further investigation we realized it was too high up the building and to irregular.

Shadows were also reported on the staircase. But it wasn't until later that we found something unusual.

A guest who was new to ghost hunts had felt something behind him but didn't want to report it. He had felt a sharp pain in his left side but carried on. It wasn't until the end of the group callout he had looked under his shirt and he had quite a nasty scratch. Regulars to The Castle Keep will know this has happened on numerous investigations and the person affected is always standing in the same area when it happens.

We have also verified this activity has happened with

other paranormal groups that have investigated The Keep in the past.

The Condemned Man's Cell:
Up the steps of the basement's Garrison there is a small room. It was where anyone that was condemned to death was placed. There is also the pit in the room where they would throw the bodies down. Hopefully you were dead or died from the fall, otherwise you would die slowly in the pit from your injuries or the local rabid dogs or rats who would help themselves from the pile of bodies.

Because of the space we are limited on how many people we can put in the room at any one time.
Through the night we placed seven different groups of people in the Cell and everyone reported the exact same activity.

All the groups reported clear tapping and banging from beneath them.

We had five different people report hearing a girl's scream. And many reported temperature drops in the area.

We had guests who had to walk out of the room as they become overcome with emotions and the feeling of hopelessness.

We set up a LiveLink (It can be seen on our Facebook page).

During the recording, you can clearly hear banging

from below us. When we used the lettered dice, we received numerous swear words including a word meaning to be beaten or tortured in response to the question," How did you die?"

Conclusion:
Another night of mystery in the heart of Newcastle. The LiveLink broadcast some very strange noises and responses.

7 JEDBURGH JAIL
ROXBURGHSHIRE

Although not officially in the North East, Jedburgh Jail was the first location we added when we decided to launch GHOSTscotland, and this now runs alongside GHOSTnortheast for our Ghosties north of The Border.

Our early research showed many reports of paranormal activity that has led many groups up the hill and through the gates of this truly foreboding location.

It has featured on many TV shows including "Most Haunted" such is its reputation for hauntings.
The history of this location is fascinating.

The town of Jedburgh lies just 10 miles from the Scottish and English border and takes its name for Jedwater, the river it stands upon.

Records date back to the ninth century when Ecgred of Lindisfarne founded a church.

A priory was built in 1147; and the ruins still stand today and can be seen as you enter the town from the south.

With it being located near the borders, Jedburgh endured hundreds of years of violence and was central to many wars between Scotland and England. In 1174 King David I built a castle on top of the hill which would eventually be demolished as the last remaining English stronghold on Scottish soil in 1409. This is the site of the current Jedburgh Jail.

The current building was built in 1823 as a prison. It was built as part of The Howard Reform of the prison service. It offered separate heated blocks for men, woman and children. There was also an exercise yard and Gaoler's House, all of which can be seen today.

Where do we investigate?
GHOSTnortheast investigates four main areas of the location covering the four main buildings. All the buildings have an upstairs and a ground floor.

East Wing:
The East Wing is where we base our Hub. The ground floor is split into two rooms. The larger area was where the prisoners were held before being moved into their cells. We have had many reports of whispering in this area, and we also have had reports of loud bangs coming from the door between the two

rooms. At one investigation, a gentleman had come away from his group as he was feeling uneasy, and he was sitting in the Hub with a team member when they heard a series of loud bangs in the room with them. We still have no explanation for them.

Upstairs we run several experiments. One of the more successful ones is when we lock one member of the group in a cell and the rest of the group gather in another cell, then callout for the lone person to be affected. On several occasions the lone guest has reported feeling the exact feeling the group has asked for. We have ruled out any noise pollution with recordings and as we use random people and random feelings we can rule out any suggestion.

Doors have been reported to slam shut on their own and footsteps on the stairwell are often reported when no-one is in the area.

West Wing:
The West Wing is a long corridor with several cells on either side. Again, this building has a ground and upper floor.

Two cells in this building are known to produce some very strange activity. I don't want to share the cell numbers as it could influence people on future investigation, with this in mind, I'll refer them to the upstairs and downstairs cells.

The downstairs cell has on numerous occasions seemed to affect people's legs. On one investigation, we had to remove four people from separate groups as they all reported that their legs were extremely painful and couldn't stand. These people were perfectly fine as soon as they had left the building. I can verify that none had knowledge of what had happened to each other.

The Upstairs seems just as strange. We get a build-up on The EMF Meters and K-2s before people burst into tears with no explanation. Strangely this does seem to affect woman a lot more than the men. Again, as soon as we remove these people from location they stop crying and feel normal. Every person who has witnessed this phenomenon have all reported seeing or feeling a young girl in the room just before crying. Indeed, we have filmed an investigation when female voices were captured on film with no explanation to where they came from. (Recording is available on our YouTube Channel).

The Men's Block:
Whether it's psychological because you know it's were the men were held or it is what still resides in the block, the men's block still feels the most un-nerving area of the location. Again, this area is split over two floors. Just like the East Wing it is a long corridor with cells either side.

We have now recorded four different reports of actual physical harm in this area. We have two reports of scratching, and both times the marks look extremely similar in size and appearance. On both these occasions the guests involved reported feeling a burning sensation before revealing large scratches on their skin.

We were filming during one claim and the recording shows that the guest did not touch himself at all so could not have caused this injury himself.

The other two incidents concern the feeling of someone grabbing their arms. The next day bruising has appeared on the victim's arms. Again both people are unconnected but the injury has shown up on the same arm.

Also, reported in this area on several occasions is a figure of a large man. I have indeed been present when three men left the location due to be feeling totally unnerved by what they described as a large dark figure who started to walk down the corridor towards them and they felt extremely threatened.

Gaoler's House:
The Gaoler's House is the main part of the museum with several exhibitions on display. We investigate the upstairs rooms that would have been bedrooms in the days of the jail.

We have used the Planchette in this area with mixed responses. The most successful piece of equipment used in this area is the Frank's Box.

We have had names that are linked to Jail over the box. Also, we have recorded extremely bad language over the box with words that I'm not sure you are even allowed to broadcast!

On several occasions when this is heard the name "Steve" is reported. I'm always asked to join the groups and on numerous occasions when I've arrived, I've been met with a barrage of abusive words. Is this merely a coincidence?

Conclusion:

Jedburgh Jail is one of the most fascinating locations we visit and we must thank Elliot who has been the "keeper of the keys" there for 17 years. His knowledge and help have been invaluable.

Visit during the day and look around at the fantastic museum and see what life was like nearly 200 years ago.

But then make sure you return when the lights go out and night creeps down the corridors and into the cells and you feel the sense of despair people must have felt.

The investigations we have conducted over the past couple of years have left me without answers to any of the questions the nights have posed. How does someone show a scratch when on video nothing is touching him? What keeps shutting doors in areas when there is no-one there? There are not many locations that I fear, but Jedburgh is top of the list!

DIARIES OF THE INVESTIGATIONS.

Investigation #1:

GHOSTnortheast travelled North of the Border to investigate the now notorious Jedburgh Jail. We only started investigating this location last year but it has fast become a firm favourite with the team and guests alike.

It was an extremely warm and clear night without a breath of wind as we started our group callout in the Men's Block.

After a short while we started to get a banging noise. It seemed to respond to request and at first, we all thought it was the cell door. We sent our Hub Manager, David and a guest into the cell to investigate but the banging stopped. On closer inspection the banging seemed to be coming from a boarded window. The board did move creating a banging noise when pushed with your hand. However, it is on the second floor so that ruled out any outside influence. There was no-one in the room when the banging was heard (witnessed by all guests) which ruled out the possibility of movement from inside the cell. The only normal explanation would be the wind. But, as I mentioned at the start, there was not a breeze or draught at this time. The noises were all caught on our video camera and we cannot explain why or how this banging seemed to respond to questions. Could it merely by a coincidence?

Another strange occurrence that was reported by

several guests was concerning the peepholes in the doors. Light shone through them naturally from inside the cells, but people were regularly reporting that the light stopped, as if being blocked from inside the cell.

The Gaoler's House.

It seemed very quiet in the Gaoler's House, with both group not reporting much activity. We did try various experiments in this area including the Planchette, Frank's Box and Scrying but with little success.

Women's Block:

During a callout in one of the cells, Group One had a series of happenings that all seemed to happen at once.

The group were calling out when one of the female guests became highly distressed for no apparent reason and had to leave. As soon as she left the room, she calmed down instantly. At the same time, we had to remove one of the male guests as he was becoming very agitated and aggressive. When we asked him, what was wrong he said he could not remember us being in the room. The group then radioed for me to help us out as one of the Teamleaders started to feel faint and sick which led to her leaving the room. The numbers had dramatically dropped inside the cell.

Group Two then conducted a similar experiment in the same cell without any knowledge of what had happened to the previous group. The guests reported the room seemed to go dark and one of the men's faces seemed to change. This man also reported the feeling of anger but said he could continue.

Both Groups also recorded low to high fluxes on the EMF Meter and had the K-2 Meter lighting up.
Apart from this cell no other activity was reported within this block.

Debtors Block.
As we use this area as our Hub, we must rule out some noise pollution from kettles and the team making the teas just before breaktime.

Group One reported very little activity, although a guest seemed to get a response on the Dowsing Rods. As this seemed to be a personal message, we will not publish the results.

Group Two also had a quiet night in this area. But there were reports of footsteps coming from outside the cells. We cannot confirm or deny that this could have been noise pollution from activity downstairs in the Hub.

Men's Block.
Group One reported activity of various amounts depending where they were. Upstairs, everyone was feeling extremely uneasy so the group decided to move downstairs, but the unease carried on.

When calling out downstairs voices were heard as if they were coming from upstairs although it was proved no-one was there. The group then seem to suffer from mass hysteria with 2 guests reporting they felt drunk. This led to 3 members having to leave the area to regain their composure.

Group Two also ended up downstairs as many of the group felt too uncomfortable to stay in the upstairs corridor.

The group carried out a callout with everyone gathered in one cell except for two female members who stayed in the main area.

The ladies were using K-2 and EMF meters. During the calling out, we recorded EMF fluxes that did seem to respond to questioning. The gauge seemed to peak when we asked if it was a male and when we mentioned stealing. We asked several controlled questions that did not get a response, but when we returned to our original questions it peaked again. Could have this been an inmate from the past?

At the end of the call out, the group gathered in the corridor area. During this time, a white light was reported to be moving at the end of the room, although we did not capture anything on our video cameras.

As we came to the end of investigating this area, one of the ladies in the group let out a scream as she was convinced she had seen a shadow move towards her, and it left her visibly shaken. What was interesting was the way she described the movement of the shadow. Her natural shadow should have moved away from her due to the light source but she described it as, moving towards her.

Overall, Jedburgh delivered a very good night with similar activity in most areas. The banging during the first group call out is some of the best activity I have witnessed but I can still not rule out a natural cause, (although I know there was no draught).

Investigation #2:

Our final visit of the year to Jedburgh was a wild and windy affair. After our arrival, the wind seemed to pick up strength although the night stayed dry. With the high winds, we immediately stated we would discount a lot of noises and banging tonight due to the draughts caused inside such an old building
.

We started as usual with our group callout in the Men's Block. After discounting numerous bangs from a couple of cells, guests started to report the feeling of getting touched. It wasn't until later that we realised it only seemed to be the female guests who were being affected. One lady reported being extremely scared as she thought she had seen a face behind another guest, which upset her as she described it as "horrible."

We brought a close to the callout and the group split up.

Debtors Block:
2 groups reported growling noises in this location. Both groups were in the upstairs area when guests reported the sound. Also, two guests were put in a cell away from their group. The group then asked for

the guests that were isolated to be touched on their right arms. Initially the 2 guests reported feeling nothing on their return until one guest noticed a red mark going around his right wrist.

Numerous banging noises were reported downstairs.

Gaoler's House:
We had set up the Frank's Box in this location and we had some very surprising responses.

Here are some of the highlights that were recorded:
Group One:
Do you know anyone in the room?
"Steve"
Steve is not in the room; do you know Steve?
"Friend."
Do you know anyone else?
"Peter." followed by "David."
Usually I would put several names down to radio broadcast but this session named all 3 male team members. Could this just be coincidence?
Group Two:
Do you have a message?
"Steve."
Do you want to speak to Steve?
"Yes."
This was then followed by a serious of swear words that can be verified by all guests that were present. As my name had been mentioned, I went to join the experiment. On my arrival, there were another two swear words clearly heard by the group. I asked,
"How many people are in the room?"
"Ten." Indeed, I was in the doorway outside and there

were 10 people. I then stepped into the room.
"How many now?"
"11."

Men's Block

During an experiment of putting people into a particular cell, three of the men in a group all started coughing and had to leave the cell in question. One described a tightening around the neck, whilst another felt sick. We then repeated this with the next group who I can verify did not know what had happened. One of the two male guests became distressed and said he felt a hand covering his mouth, he then had to leave the location and did not return.

Conclusion:

Jedburgh delivered again with some very unusual activity that was being replicated in every group. The Frank's Box activity was quite extraordinary.

Investigation #3:

As we enter Jedburgh Jail I always get a feeling of hesitation and anxiety. It's foreboding position on top the hill overlooking the village below and its proximity to the large cemetery also doesn't help the feeling of being watched as you enter the gates.

We had mixed weather during the night, as we encountered some heavy rain. Then the night cleared up to a perfect night sky full of stars. The wind was blustery so some of the recorded noises have been discounted as we cannot rule out natural causes.

We started the night off upstairs in the Men's Block for our group callout.

During the callout guests were reporting feeling cold and some reported being touched. Several noises were recorded starting with a gentle tapping before thuds and a bang was heard within the block. One person reported that they felt as something was grabbing their wrist and it hurt. We examined the persons' arm at numerous times of the night, and it did seem red (but nothing of note.) The next morning, I was contacted by the person with a photograph showing the area badly bruised. This is not the first time we have had physical harm in this location. This will be the fourth time it's been reported and every time it is in the same area of the same arm.

Also, during the group callout several of the guests reported hearing a growling noise that couldn't be explained naturally.

Women's Block:
Not a lot of activity to report from the women's block. 2 of the groups got very similar activity on both the EMF Meters and K-2 Meters. This is a regular occurrence which would usually lead you to believe that something natural was causing the fluctuations. However, every baseline check before and after the investigations show no natural electricity source in the cells that we use.

One group reported hearing heavy footsteps outside the cell they were in and at the same time darkness under the door, as if someone was walking past. When they opened the door expecting to see a guest or team member, no-one was present. This happened on two occasions.

Men's Block:
The Men's Block seems to be delivering the same activity time and time again.

In the upstairs corridor, all groups reported hearing footsteps and tapping. One guest was put into a cell by themselves but left the room extremely quickly reporting something standing so close in front of her she could feel it's breath on her face.

Temperature changes were also reported in this area but the reads were inconclusive.

Debtors Block:
As with the men's block all the reported activity was reported in the upstairs cells. One group got some good responses when using pendulums which did give us a name and age that does correspond with a known prisoner that was indeed kept in the Debtor's Block.

There were also reports of footsteps out in the corridor but no-one was found when the groups investigated further.

Gaoler's House:
We always use our Frank's Box experiment in this location and we are now building quite a large database of references that are being heard over the box.

Again, on this investigation we recorded several obscenities that we are still unaware of being allowed to be broadcast over the radio.

Again, as in past investigations they seem to revolve around the name Steve. "Steve" and "David" have now been recorded on 90% of all our investigations at Jedburgh Jail, followed by a series of swear words.

However, when David and I are called for, the box seems to go quiet with nothing more heard. When we left the words began again.

Are we reading too much into what could clearly be a coincidence or is there something trying to communicate their feelings about some of our team members.

Conclusion:
Altogether a quieter night than usual at Jedburgh, however the bruising of the man's arm is still leaving us with questions at a location that is starting to get a reputation for physical harm. The Frank's Box constantly amazes me with the same words being said time and again but only at this location.

Investigation #4:

After our summer break, we headed North to Jedburgh for our first investigation of the Autumn/Winter Season.

On the journey, we were treated to the rare sight of clear skies as it was the first time in two years of investigating the Jail that we did not have to travel through the rain. The night was perfect for ghost hunting as there was no moon to distort any light and the night was completely still without any wind. However, the mood was to change as the night got started in one of our most infamous locations.

Men's Block:

We started the night with a group callout in the Men's Block. The group reported muffled voices, footsteps and noises coming from inside the cells upstairs. Also, many of the group were reporting seeing shadows moving at the bottom of the corridor. We tried to find a natural explanation for the movement but we couldn't.

The groups then split up.

During the night, all three groups reported a guest being pushed in the Men's Block. All three guests were unrelated to each other and had not shared their experiences until the end of the night.

Two of the groups recorded doors being slammed downstairs, however I confirmed all doors were shut. One group had asked if whoever was in the building could affect somebody in the next group by touching their left arm as they were leaving. A lady from the next group then reported that she felt as if something had pulled her left arm sharply. Had something delivered the first groups request?

A gentleman volunteered to do a lone vigil in the Men's Block. He was left alone in the Block, only to ask to leave during the experiment as he had heard a mumbled voice or groan from the stairwell. Fortunately, we had placed a video camera in the location and on playback you can hear a loud moan just as the guest had described. We can verify there was no-one else in the building at this time. This coincided with what had been reported earlier in the night.

Women's Block:
The Women's Block only seemed to deliver any activity to one group and ironically it was the only group of all women. They reported activity on the Dowsing Rods which gave us answers to questions that did correspond to previous investigations. They also reported hearing noises coming from one particular cell, but nothing was there when they looked.

Debtor's Block:
The Debtor's Block probably delivers the consistent activity in this location. Again, the team reported various noises and occurrences in two of the cells. The cell and it's noises have been reported over 12 times on previous hunts and seem to tell a story about the Jail. Once again, as with previous hunts here, we

had to remove a guest from the cell as they seemed overcome with emotions.

Gaoler's House:

We conduct the Planchette and the Frank's Box experiments here. Although the Planchette seemed to be quiet on the night without anything of note to report, the Frank's Box was a different story!

All three groups recorded the name Steve on numerous occasions during their vigils. Regular magazine readers and visitors to Jedburgh will know this seems to happen on every night we attend the Jail. Once again we asked the box how many people were in the room during the callouts. The box responded with 11. There were indeed 11 people there, including the team members.

The third group reported what is also becoming a regular occurrence on the Box. After certain questions, all the guests in the group heard a barrage of swear words, including some extremely offensive words. As far as we are aware we can't think of any radio channel that would allow these words to be broadcast, even at such a late hour?

Conclusion:

A great start to the new season and Jedburgh delivered again. The place gets darker with every visit and seems to want to tell its stories.

Investigation #5:

The evening had started cold and wet but as the night started the clouds had cleared away to leave a perfect sky and very little wind. The wind speeds are always calculated at this location so we can rule out natural draughts and breezes.

We started the night with our group callout, when we experienced some unusual activity. First, the far corridor seemed to go darker near to the window as if someone was moving around. Then we heard banging downstairs, which described as doors being closed. Everyone in the building was accounted for, so we have no explanation as to how the doors moved by themselves.

Men's Block:

Again, the men's block was to deliver the most activity. We had several guests both male and female having to leave this area due to either fear or feeling ill.

Voices were heard within the upstairs cells. These were reported by all three separate groups, and guests said they seemed to resonate from the cells, although again no explanation could be given for them.

In the upstairs corridor, several guests from a group reported seeing orbs of light cross into a cell. This is unusual as orbs tend to be seen on camera. All the guests reported seeing the same lights in the same area?

Gaoler's House:
We tried the Scrying Mirrors in this area and we had some very interesting results.

Seven different guests described seeing the exact same thing in the mirrors. The description was in line with what we have had reported in the past in this area.
Looking at some of the photographs taken, they do show distortion on several guests faces.

One group had an interesting Frank's Box session. Several of the answers to our controlled questions were direct hits with information about several of the former prisoners and coincide with some of our previous investigations. Are these names and dates purely coincidence, or can we say after six and seven times, it is something more than that?

Women's Block:
The Women's Block was inactive for most people. One group did get some information through when using the pendulum. Unfortunately, the information they gathered cannot be verified.

Debtor's Wing:
Two of our groups reported several bangs upstairs when they were in the cells. They said that they were expecting a someone to be in the corridor when they came out but CCTV can prove that no-one was in the entire block at the time, never mind the corridor. It did leave several guests shaken by the experience as the noise had been quite loud.

Conclusion:

Overall Jedburgh seemed quieter than usual, however when we put the reports together the three groups seemed to be experiencing the exact same activity in the same places.

The Jail is creating quite a sizeable file on information that always matches information that we have gathered in the past. The same names and numbers seem to appear over and again, whilst the noises and movements are in the same areas.

Investigation #6:

We started the night with a group callout in The Men's Block.

The corridor was lighter than usual as the summer sun was starting to set, but the corridor got darker as the callout went on.

Numerous taps were heard around the cells but nothing really of note. The group then heard a door shut downstairs below us. When we went to look, there was no-one there but one of the cell doors was shut. (We had opened them all before the callout.) There were also reports of shadows moving right in front of guests. This was witnessed by several people, as the moving shadow was in the centre of the group.

The Debtors Wing:
A lot of activity centred around one cell. Two of the three groups all reported seeing a small figure in the cell, the size of a child. This has been reported on previous visits. One guest reported being touched on the hand, then become extremely emotional and had to leave the group and spend time in the hub area.

Men's Block:
Shadows moving at the bottom of the corridor was reported several times during the night along with murmurings and whispers.

We had a total of three guests leave the Men's Block during the night as they were feeling claustrophobic and scared, as if something was intimidating them out of the building.

Again, a door was heard being slammed along the corridor, unfortunately we cannot verify if the door was open before we started.

K-2 and EMF Meters were showing fluctuations especially when the word "Guard" was used. This has us intrigued as there is no electricity in that building to cause any fluctuations.

Women's Block:
The Pendulum experiment was the most successful in this block, with all the groups reporting getting responses to questions on it. Everything seemed to indicate a woman and a child within the walls. We are still investigating the names and information that was given to us, to see if it is traceable.

Gaoler's House:
Unusually the Frank's Box experiment was very quiet tonight. The Planchette also didn't give us much activity either.

Conclusion:
Another active night in one of our most foreboding locations. A lot of the activity is in line with previous visits. An unusually quiet Gaoler's House but a very active Debtor's Block shows that we can never second guess where and what is going to happen.

Investigation #7:

I always enjoy the drive to Jedburgh. It only takes an hour from Newcastle and you drive up through the Cheviots and some of the most beautiful scenery in the world, especially if you have time to stop off at Carter's Bar. Although, at this time of the year it is dark and once you pass Otterburn, the roads start to get exceptionally dark. However, it was a fine night with plenty of moonshine and the no hint of the rain we usually encounter.

We started the night with a good mixture of new members and regular guests gathering in the Men's Block for a group callout.

Noises were reported around the group from the sounds of people muttering to footsteps in the corridors. A real feeling of uneasiness developed in the block as people reported seeing dark figures moving in front of them. Noises were heard in the stairwell and we stopped waiting for someone to arrive, but no-one was there. We had people describing fluctuations in temperature, although our logger recorded a constant 18 degrees throughout the call out. We tried using a Scot to call out, but even this didn't provoke a reaction.

Gaoler's House:

We used several different experiments in this building. We use the planchette and Frank's Box as they seem to deliver the best results.

Not a lot was reported on the Planchette from any of the groups but the Frank's Box seemed to deliver the usual responses.

We had three names that came out with some of the groups that we can confirm that have been used in previous visits. These were first names, which can be linked to Jedburgh, and one is quite unique.

The request to speak to Steve followed by several swear words was reported by two guests and is now becoming a consistent response in this location. When I come into the room, the box says several very offensive swear words then goes quiet. Is this a coincidence? It has now happened on 93% of our visits over the past five years.

Women's Block:

The Woman's Block has its fair share of activity and it also seems to revolve around the same cells. These both seem to deliver the same sort of activity and it was repeated again tonight.

Voices are reported in these areas, but they often described as seeming to be a conversation between people.

Two groups reported hearing this and on both occasions, we had to check where everyone was. All team and guests were accounted for and were not around these two teams when they heard the voices.
We captured this on video, and it can be seen on our YouTube Channel.

One of the teams reported heavy footsteps outside in the corridor while they were conducting a vigil. No-one is outside in this corridor and this was verified by our video equipment.

Debtor's Block:
The Debtor's Block gave the teams some unusual activity and this was probably best captured on our LiveLink.

All three groups reported that their pendulum experiments delivered results., indicating that there had been both children and females in the area.

We had several reports of EMF fluctuations even though all electrics were switched off in the area at the time.
However, it was one cell that caused the most discussion. I won't say which one so we can see if this happens on further investigations. In this cell two of

the three groups reported hearing footsteps outside and seeing the light changing under the door as if someone had walked past. There was a feeling of unease and dread that led to several members leaving the room.

Indeed, during our weekly LiveLink, Marty and I went into this same cell to see what would happen whilst we were broadcasting live. Our viewers clearly saw and confirmed that the shadows at the back of the wall moved as if something had shifted. This was followed by a noise that I can only explain as a growl. Not an animal growl, but it sounded as if someone was angry with us.

Conclusion:

I think by the end of the night there were some very shaken people. Although no-one had been physically harmed, I think there was enough going on in Jedburgh Jail for you to ask," What's just happened?" Let's hope we find out next time.

Investigation #8:

It was a clear night with a very large bright moon lighting the way. It was getting colder as you could feel winter starting to bite but it wasn't cold enough to make the night uncomfortable.

We settled in the Men's Block for the group callout and to get the night started.

After investigating this location so many times the team seem unaffected with the activity that is reported by guests. Is it with the same reports on every investigation that we have stopped asking if it's coincidence?

Dark shadows of what was described as a large man were reported within the corridors. Temperature fluctuations were recorded. With a group of people in a small space the expectations would be for reports of people warming up, but the reports were of drops in certain areas.

We split into smaller groups to investigate the location and weren't expecting to witness a photograph that has left us stunned.

Men's Block:
All three of our groups reported activity in this area. Footsteps were recorded on both the ground floor and upstairs corridors. Doors were reported being closed in areas where we had nobody present.

As readers of our magazine and indeed regular guests will know, we have had people physically hurt in this area and tonight we would witness this activity again.

A lady who had reported feeling uneasy and seeing a large shadow near her then reported pains in her neck. She described it as a burning sensation. When we removed her scarf, it revealed a rather nasty scratch mark. Now we can't 100% verify this was paranormal but it was in the exact same place as our previously scratched guests.

During the night one lady had been taking photographs in the upstairs corridor of the Men's Block and she asked us to look at her phone.

The photograph seemed to resemble a man in a hat and to be honest at first seemed too good to be true! The lady sent us the original photo and we have spent several hours looking at it.

We can rule out natural effects such as shadows, as parts of the figure are transparent. Plus, the flash would have shown the figure in front of the camera. We have tried everything including various light and photo filters, but have not come up with an explanation for it.

The group in question had not reported anything unusual at the time the picture was taken and it was only noticed afterwards.

Debtor's Block:
The groups used the box of equipment in this area and the upstairs corridor delivered some positive responses on both the EMF Meters and the Pendulum. One group were convinced someone was in the building with them, but as we investigated further it was proven that they were on their own.
They reported footsteps from the bottom of the corridor and what sounded like the doors opening.

Gaoler's House:
The Gaoler's House seemed like a repeat of our earlier visits.

The Planchette seemed to be quieter and one group reported it only moved when the male guests were using it. The Frank's Box broadcast its usual string of abusive words followed by the same names that we have had in the past. Some of the guests experimented with the Scrying Mirrors. Three of them reported seeing changes on their faces and they all described the same features.

Conclusion:

Jedburgh Jail is showing the same activity on every visit. It's starting to become hard to ask if this coincidence. We will be following the activity closely on future visits.

8 THE BUFFALO CENTRE
BLYTH

You can find the Buffalo Centre in the heart of The Port of Blyth in Northumberland.

This building has quite a history and has had various uses which we will discover.

Firstly, the building can be found in Cowpen area of Blyth and is near to the Quayside of the River Blyth. Being a harbour town, the history of Blyth goes back centuries and Blyth itself hides some hidden secrets of days gone by.

Although not confirmed, it is believed that a settlement in Blyth dates to Neanderthal Times; This is due to local findings of such items as copper axes and knives. It is thought that the Romans had a camp at Freehold Street which is a few hundred yards away from The Buffalo.

The first signs of a settlement dates to 1130, with the town seeming to have grown around it's river and harbour. Today Blyth still is a bustling market town
.

Not much more is mentioned until the 17th Century. During the following 300 years, the town boomed through the industrial revolution as it's fishing and local coal mines saw the town become an important part of the North East.

The Buffalo Centre is currently a community centre and provides some excellent services for the local community. It has two main floors and third floor that serves as a flat for the caretaker. Outside in the back area is a small one storey building which is where the original stables stood. They were linked to a coaching inn and can be traced back to late 17th Century. The main building was rebuilt in 1899 due to a fire that destroyed the original building and is now easily recognisable due to its Victorian architecture.

During the past 300 years, the buildings on this site have been used as a coaching inn, hotel, shops, housing and during the majority of the 20th Century, a public house.

It has been a quite hard and time consuming to obtain a lot of information about its past and the stories of its previous occupants. However, this has made our investigations a lot more exciting.

Where do we investigate?
We investigate three main areas of this location; Both public floors in the main building, and the old stables area.

The Stable Block:
This building is probably the most consistent of the three areas. It is split into 3 small rooms. The first larger room we use for group callouts and various team experiments.

We have had reports during the callouts of people hearing footsteps or banging upstairs. However, the modern building has no upstairs, although our research has found that the original building did indeed have a second floor.

Also in this area, numerous independent witnesses have reported seeing a large dark figure in the corner of the room making them feel extremely uncomfortable. On occasion, they have been so scared they had to leave. The Stables have also witnessed an incident we were lucky enough to capture on video, where an item we believe was a coin was thrown across the room. The video is on YouTube and we have reviewed it many times but still cannot explain where the coin came from. Reports of temperature fluctuations and feelings of anger are often reported in this area too.

In the second, smaller room, we conduct the Ouija Board experiment. It does seem to be very active here but most messages seem to be of a personal nature (GHOSTnortheast never share or publish personal messages). We did witness one occasion where it spelled out a name and an event that was linked to the building. After many months of careful research we did verify the link and the information that we received was all correct (including the name and dates).

Main Building Downstairs:

One of the most impressive examples of activity witnessed in the downstairs hall was when 9 guests saw a chair move across the floor. They reported seeing it move about three feet across the room and stop.

The witnesses included both guests and team, and it is consistent with reports of activity given by the residents of the Buffalo.

We have witnessed many EMF fluctuations in this room, but it always seems to focus around young people both male and female.

We conduct the Frank's Box experiment in this room. The most impressive session was a night when all three groups reported hearing the exact same message relating to a fishing accident. Unfortunately, we have been unable to link the information to any known incident. However, we will keep researching as it mentioned specifics with words that are not often broadcast over the radio.

We have also had many sessions on the Box repeatedly using bad language. This always seems to be focused towards women and the use of derogatory comments towards them and are always spoken in a male voice.

Main Building Upstairs:

Upstairs is split into two main areas that we use. The first is a small room at the rear of the building and the second is the main exercise hall.

First is the small room, where we conduct our Planchette experiment. We have had varying results over the past few years, from nothing at all, to an occasion where we ran out of paper as the Planchette seemed to go into overdrive! Most of the messages in the past have been of personal note and as always GHOSTnortheast never share anything personal.

One night stands out in this room. The Planchette was not active at all, however the EMF Meter was fluctuating, but only around one chair. This had been sat on but the temperature was noticeably lower on it than anywhere in the room. Having been sat on, this chair should have been warmer like the other chairs in the room.

We know there is a link with a child in this room and a guest suggested that a child wouldn't be able to reach the table where the Planchette was placed. We then placed the experiment on the floor and within minutes we started to get a response.

We try many different experiments in the second room. On several occasions we've conducted group callouts here, and have recorded strange tapping coming from the floor and the walls that seem to respond to request.

Footsteps and mumbling have also been reported in this room when there is no-one else around.

We also use our Scrying Mirrors here. We have had many reports of the exact same face being described in this room and links with the reports of a boy wandering through the upstairs rooms.

I remember one of our regular guests (an experienced investigator) trying Scrying for the first time. It was to be his last. To this day, he still has not shared what he saw, but he left the room and hasn't returned to the location since. He has also refused to do any form of Scrying since.

Conclusion:
A normal building on a normal street, but once it's dark inside the atmosphere is far from normal. The modern interior fools you into forgetting the years of history the building is standing on. It has delivered some of the most unusual activity we have witnessed from flying coins to the doors flying open.

DIARIES OF THE INVESTIGATIONS.

Investigation #1:

We usually conduct our "Night of Victorian Séance," at this location but tonight we were teaming up for another fundraiser with members of the public who were raising funds for a local charity called P.A.R.R.T. who are an animal rescue service based in Northumberland.

We arrived at the location on an overcast but warm summers evening and after the mandatory health and safety briefing we moved to the Stable area for our full group callout.

During the callout, we had guests reporting dark shadows in various parts of the room, with one particular female guest becoming invisible from the neck up because of the darkness. It was also noted by several of the guests that her appearance was changing. They all reported that she looked bald and her face was distorted. The guest involved reported that she was feeling extremely warm but other guests said there was a cold draught.

Also reported throughout the callout was a feeling of being intimidated by two of the group, whilst another lady said she felt extreme anger and at one point wanted to "hit" me when I spoke!

All these reports are consistent with the incidents in this area that we have logged over the past 3 years of investigating this location.

Ground Floor
We set up The Frank's Box experiment in the main community room.

Group One were first to try it. The following is a transcript of what was recorded:
What is your name? - No response
What was your job? - Pimp
Did you say pimp? - Yes
Who are you? - No response
Did you live here? - No response
Why are you here? - Girls
Our girls? - No
Do you know anybody? - Steve
At this point the group called for me to join them.
Is this the Steve you know? - No response
Do you have a message for Steve? - No response
Do you like Steve? - Aww yes.
This brought much laughter from the group.

During the questions, the EMF Meter was constantly moving from 1mg to 4mg but only when questions were being asked.

With the responses in mind we wrote down several questions for the second group to ask but did not give them any specific information on what had just been said in the room.

Group Two soon started with the Frank's Box. Again, this is a transcript of what was recorded:
What's your name? - Ashley
How old are you? - 24
Can you confirm your name? - No response

Are you 24? - Aye
What was your job? - Singer
The group were talking between themselves and discussing the answers when all the group heard an expletive from The Frank's Box.
Did you say "expletive?" - Yes
Are you a man or a woman? - Man
What's your name? - Steve.
When did you die? - 78
The Group asked a few more questions but nothing of note was recorded.

With both groups getting similar answers (and an expletive heard that I know doesn't get broadcast on British radio), who were they talking to?

1st Floor
Upstairs the groups tried various experiments including the Planchette, Dowsing Rods and Pendulum. Some activity was reported but none of the information given can be confirmed.

The groups then tried Scrying Mirrors. A few guests reported seeing things but had nothing significant to report.

During a later group callout, we tried an audio experiment without much success, although two of the guests and team member had to leave the room after feeling dizziness and nausea. These feeling were totally unexplained as the room was cool, but they are consistent with previous experiences in this area.

The Stables.

Group One tried the Ouija board. There was no response, so they moved into the main area and gathered around the table to conduct a séance. During the séance a coin appeared to be thrown in the top corner of the room.

Looking back at the video recording, it shows no-one in the room moving at the time when the coin makes 2 impact noises. (What I presume as the noises made by the coin hitting the wall then the floor). However, I cannot see any flight of the coin on the recording. The video can be viewed on YouTube.

Group Two reported no activity on the Ouija board. However, during the time in this location the group did report hearing male voices on two separate occasions. On further investigation, there was no-one around the building, but we cannot rule out for definite that it didn't come from outside.

Overall, a quieter night at The Buffalo, although the words on the Frank's Box were very impressive. Also, looking at the coin hitting the floor, I can't rule out the fact it could have simply fallen out of someone's pocket but you can clearly hear two sounds of impact on the video which suggests to me that it hits the wall first.

Investigation #2:

We started our night in the Stables area for our group callout. It started with a few taps and shadow movement reported by a few of the guests. Then after 15 minutes into the callout I asked if any spirit could replicate me banging. I clapped my hands loud twice loudly. A loud banging replied within seconds. Every guest in the room can verify this loud noise and we captured it on video. What created this noise? We are still unsure.

Also, reports of what sounded like footsteps coming up the metal ramp outside were reported and this was to be a feature of the night. Every time we checked, no-one was there. We also tried to replicate the noise, but to no avail. Just before we broke off noises were reported from upstairs. This has been reported many times before only for us to show the guests that the modern building doesn't have an upper level.

First floor Main Building:

This area gave us the most activity via the Planchette and EMF Meters. With one group, a gentleman guest reported feeling as if something had brushed against him. The EMF reacted but only around this guest and only up to his waist. After questions were asked the group had a sense it was a spirit of a child. The Planchette had not moved but it was suggested if it was a child it wouldn't be able to reach. The group then moved the Planchette to the floor, where it did appear to move. Could this be paranormal or simply suggestion? Also, in the area of the EMF activity we measured an increase of 4 degrees in temperature but only this particular spot.

Ground Floor:

We experimented with the Frank's Box in this area. A group did report some very unusual responses from the box including some very questionable language. It seemed to follow on from our previous investigation, with a very similar theme aimed at one guest.

Some of the answers given link with the history of the Buffalo when it was a public house.
We also used The Ouija Board in this area received numerous personal messages.

Conclusion:

Another night at the Buffalo with activity similar to that which has been reported in the past. The Stable area still seems the strangest part of the location, however this time, the upstairs of the main building certainly came to life. Does someone want to communicate with the Frank's Box or is it merely coincidence?

Investigation #3:

It was a clear mild night and we were joined by a good mix of new and regular guests.

We started our group callout in the Stables area of the location.

During a relevantly quiet start to the callout we started to experience some noises around the room. A regular tapping was heard. At first, we thought was coming from outside but were unable to track the source. A shadowy figure was reported in the far end of the room where we have had similar reports in the past. We also had a guest reporting that I called out, they become extremely agitated and angry. Again, this has been reported in this area several times before.

We recorded several temperature fluctuations in the room with the guests reporting feeling extremely warm one minute, then really cold the next. We couldn't explain why the temperature was constantly changing.

We also had reports of what sounded like footsteps outside but no-one was there.

The Stables Area:
We conduct the Ouija Board experiment in this area. We didn't seem to get much activity linked to the location. However, there were two sessions where people received personal messages. Also, as with the group callouts, the temperature kept showing five-degree fluctuations.

Downstairs Main Hall:
We conducted the Frank's Box in the hall. As in past investigations two of the groups reported strong swear words being heard that seemed to be directed at the younger guests and the Teamleaders. The second team asked what it had called the previous Teamleader and four out of the five words it had broadcast were repeated.

Upstairs Hall:
We tried Scrying in this area without much success so we then moved onto the Planchette. Two of the groups reported slight movement while using "yes"

and "no" cards to answer their questions. The third group was more active, with the Planchette seemingly trying to write a name. As the group tried to get a more distinctive answer, the experiment seemed to stop working. Our Teamleader asked if we were annoying them with their request, they then heard a loud bang. We took this as an answer and with respect closed the session down.

Conclusion:
A quieter than normal night at the Buffalo Centre but interesting nonetheless.

The only activity that was reported seemed to be in line with what has been seen and heard before. We were particularly interested in the temperature fluctuations as we could not find a natural source, for example a draughty door or window and we confirmed the building doesn't have air conditioning. Also, the swearing on the Frank's Box is consistent with previous nights.

Investigation #4:

We arrived at Blyth on quite a warm evening for October with no wind and a clear sky. We were armed with five different types of Ouija Boards to trial something we had never tried before. 5 Boards in one location!

The Buffalo is situated on a main road that is relevantly quiet at that time of night. The Victorian structure stands out on the corner of the road opposite the modern buildings of the Quayside and its industrial estate. The stable area dates to the 17th Century and would be interesting to think what the landscape would have looked like back then. It probably had an unblocked view looking straight down the river as it meanders down towards the sea.

The Stable Area:

Although a modern structure, this building stands exactly on the same spot as the original stables were built over 300 years ago. We conducted our group callout in this area.

The night started with a serious of bangs from above. Remember that the new structure does not have an upstairs and is a flat roofed building, unlike the original block.

Several times on request we had loud noises from above. We also reported several noises coming from the kitchen area of the stables which everyone could clearly see were empty.

As the callout continued, guests started to report feeling changes in the temperature. This was interesting as the room is centrally heated and was extremely warm. We could find no natural draughts to cause any form of temperature drops.

One of the most unusual things was reports from several guests that the appearance of one of the female guests at the top end of the room seemed to have changed. I can verify that I personally witnessed what they were seeing. They all reported that the lady seemed to be wearing a white dress similar to a bridal gown. However, when the lights came up, the lady in question was wearing a tracksuit. How had several people all reporting to see the same thing got her appearance so dramatically wrong? I can't find any link to a bride in The Buffalo's history but we are still researching Blyth's archives.

After the group callout, we split into our smaller groups to investigate. All groups reported some activity on the Ouija boards in this area. One group had some strong personal messages. One of our guests had to leave on several occasions as they seemed overwhelmed with what was going on.

Main Building Upstairs:
Again, we had Ouija Boards in place to complement the Planchette experiment, however it was one groups experience with the Scrying Mirrors that was to be more of interest. A male guest decided to use the black Scrying mirrors and his reflection seemed to change dramatically. This could be seen by others in the room, and coincided with some information gained from one of the Ouija Boards being used. Could this be a mere co-incidence or in fact were we getting two pieces of equipment both working in unison?

We also conducted a second group callout in this area later in the night. Although nothing was encountered, we did have three guests that were standing close to each other, all needing to leave.

Main Building Downstairs:

In the downstairs area of the main building we had another Ouija Board in place. However, the groups seemed to concentrate more on the Frank's Box experiment as this had been very active in this location before.

Again, as on other visits, we seemed to get words linked to the surrounding area rather than the building. We had words about boating; and fishing with "Ashington" mentioned which lies on the other side of the River Blyth. Could we have just been picking up a local radio station and making the words fit?

Also, reports of fluctuations on both EMF and K-2 Meters were recorded at different times, but they also seemed to respond to questions asked by the teams.

Conclusion:

The Buffalo is a strange location. The Stable Area seems to be the "see and feel" area of the buildings, while the main house seems to deliver the experimental side of the investigation.

Investigation #5:

As we arrived in Blyth, it was raining.

However, the weather was going to prepare us for the photographs we were about to witness!

We started with a group callout in the Stable Block. The Stables are usually an area where there is a lot of reports of noises but it was a visual that would get the guests excited.

A guest had left a torch on the table, and although it was switched off it was still luminous. The guest was going to remove it but I decided to leave it on the table and try a different approach to the callout.

I asked if anything was present could it move or blackout the object on the table.

At first guests thought it had moved but on further investigation we confirmed it hadn't, however every guest in the room reported that it looked as if the torch had disappeared, I witnessed this too. I moved around the table to observe the object from different angles and I had to agree with the guests. The object seemed to be cloaked in darkness. When I asked if it could move away from the torch so we could see it again, it seemed to reappear.

We repeated this a few times to rule out a trick of the light or our eyes, but again the light around the torch was changing in front of us.

As we watched back on the camcorder recording the room, the camera seemed to keep losing its focus in sync with reports of the darkness around the torch. The unfocused camera is becoming a regular occurrence during our investigations.

We also had three guests leave the callout as all three complained of nausea. Again, a similarity with previous investigations in this location.

Downstairs:

We conducted the Frank's Box in this area but it was photographs that was to have the whole group talking by the end of the night.

During the break, a guest brought a very strange photo to our attention that he had taken in the room. The group had been sitting at the back of the room, looking into the large mirrored wall. The gentleman's photo seems to show a figure standing to the right of the room. We asked him to email it as usual and we would take a closer look at the end of the night. (This gives us a chance to look at it closely on a big screen and with filters). However, about an hour later the Teamleader from a separate group came to me with a photograph that a lady had taken in the same room. Again, the photo showed a large shadowy figure on the right side of the room. The photos were nearly identical. However, these had been taken by two completely different people, at different times but in the same place.

I asked the gentleman to join me downstairs, I confirmed that both guests didn't know each other and had no idea what the other had captured.

I then asked them to swap photos to look at each other's photos.

Their faces were priceless as the photos were so similar.

Upstairs Hall:
Along with the Ouija Board we conducted a Scrying session in this area. Two of the groups reported some very good successes, both describing very similar results. Guests reported seeing an older man with dirty hair. Also, they reported that he looked angry. It does seem strange that several guests all used the same wording which led to three guests leaving the session upset.

Ouija Boards:
As it was "The Night of 5 Ouija Boards", it is worth mentioning we did get a lot of information throughout the night. The names "Sam" and "John" were repeated several times. Both names have been reported many times before in this location with them both being recorded on the Frank's Box in the past.

Conclusion:
A great night for activity at The Buffalo. I'm still researching all the information we were given.
But what about the photographs? Is it a guest? Is it spirit? The photographs are available on our YouTube channel.

Investigation #6:

This fantastic Victorian building is perfect to play host to a Victorian investigation and that is why the Buffalo Centre becomes "The Night of 5 Ouija Boards". We also try and do various experiments that replicate the era, although, we do try and mix them with modern day technology.

It was a mixed evening for weather as the night started clear but it did start to drizzle halfway through the night. We gathered in the Stables to start the night with the usual group callout.
The callout started nervously as several noises were reported but we found natural causes for most of them.

Noises were also reported outside on the metal ramp that leads to the door. We cannot rule out natural causes as we had no camera present, but we still don't have an explanation to what was making these noises.

As the callout got going people started to report different feelings. We had people going hot when the guests next to them were going cold. Part of the room at the back seemed to go pitch black and we couldn't see the guests who stood there. Something I witnessed along with the guests was a lady who appeared to be standing as usual. It wasn't until later we realized she was sitting and had been sitting all the time. From the other side of the room it looked like a person standing up straight.

And then the door opened!

The main door to the building is in the room that we were all gathered in. It is a modern double-glazed door, so it does need to click to close. As I mentioned earlier, we had been hearing noises outside when the door simply opened of its own accord.

Obviously, everyone in the room got a shock at this. We shut the door again and made sure it clicked into place, and we also asked a guest to double check the door was closed and secure. We started to callout again and again we heard noises on the outside ramp. We asked whoever it was to join us again, and the door opened for the second time, which did bring a few loud cries and swear words from some of the guests.

The guest near the door ran out immediately to ensure nobody was outside playing a prank, but no-one was in the area. Also, what makes this a little more confusing, is that the back area is walled and secure; For anyone to get in they would have to climb a ten-foot wall and over barbed wire. There also is a security light in the back that is motion censored. This did not turn on, on either occasion. We do not have any explanation as to what opened the door once, never mind twice. We have investigated the Buffalo for six years and the door has never done this in the past.

Ouija Boards:
As it was a night of 5 Ouija Boards, there was a Ouija Board in every location. These ranged in type and size from our round three feet large board to a A4 sized traditional board.

As with any equipment, The GHOSTnortheast team do not touch or interact with the glass. They will advise and ask questions. The guests are the only people with their fingers on the glass, also we ask guests to turn their fingers upside down so the only contact they have is the finger nail tips.

During the night, two groups reported several accounts of activity on the boards.

As most the information that came through was of a personal nature we will not publish this information. We did receive two names that are linked to area, but both are also linked to happenings that occurred in the area from a recent time. We will not publish this information as there is a possibility that there are living relatives connected to it.

Conclusion:

Seeing the door open not once but twice did leave me speechless.

I spent the rest of the night trying to work out how this could have happened naturally and I still have no natural explanation.

The Stable Area always seems to deliver activity that we cannot explain, with coins flying to doors opening on their own. Roll on our next visit.

9 JARROW HALL
SOUTH TYNESIDE

When we were offered Jarrow Hall as a new and exclusive location in September, we didn't hesitate in saying yes.

Formerly known as Bede's World, this 12-acre site was closed in February by South Tyneside Council during their spending cuts.

Since then a fantastic charity called Groundworks South Tyneside has stepped in to try and reinstall this fantastic glimpse into the past back to its former glory.

The site includes a replica Anglo Saxon Settlement complete with housing and a working farm, a museum dedicated to The Venerable Bede, and Jarrow Hall, a Georgian Town House nestled within its own grounds.

This was probably going to be our most ambitious hunt to date and with such a vast history spanning the site our research was going to be extensive. The following paragraphs just scratch the surface of the history of Jarrow Hall and the surrounding site.

Jarrow is a small town that is located on the south banks of the Tyne. But this little town that sits at the entrance/exit of The Tyne Tunnel has a very interesting past spanning over 2000 years!

In the First Century, the Romans built a settlement at Jarrow and fortified the area along with its neighbours in South Shields. Parts of the forts and settlements can still be seen today.

However, it wasn't until the 7th Century that Jarrow would make its mark in history.

In 674, Benedict Biscop built a monastery called St. Peter's on the banks of the nearby Wear to teach Christianity. Such was the success of St. Peter's, King Egfrid of Northumbria issued more land for a second monastery.

In 682, Benedict Biscop built St. Paul's and took his protégé Bede and a monk named Ceolfrith with him. Ceolfirth would later produce The Codex Amiatinus, one of three Latin Bibles he created. (One bible for each monastery and The Codex Amiatinus itself was to be presented to The Pope in Rome). Ceolfirth had planned to deliver this himself, but he died in 718 on route to Rome. His fellow monks continued the journey and eventually it was presented to Pope Gregory II.

Unfortunately, the two copies that were made for the monasteries have been lost in history but The Codex Amiatinus was found and is still housed in Tuscany, Italy. A replica of this fantastic book can now be found in the Museum at Jarrow Hall.

Bede was to go on and excel as a scholar at St. Peter's and became known as the Venerable Bede.

On his travels to Rome, he had created an extensive library of knowledge for the monasteries and before his death, he was recognised as England's leading historian.

He had penned the famous "Historia Ecclesiatica Gentis Anglorum." The book was a history of English Churches and was to form an invaluable source of research into Anglo Saxon Britain.

The museum within the Jarrow Hall Site houses a fantastic exhibition to The Venerable Bede and all his important work.

The monasteries suffered in the late 8th Century and early 9th Century from Viking raids. In fact, Jarrow was the second place in England to be attacked, following Lindisfarne.

Over the following centuries the monastery and surrounding area fell into ruin as the wars with Scotland and the dissolution of the Church by King Henry VIII finally took their toll and Jarrow went back to being a small settlement on the banks of the Tyne.

Jarrow would re-appear in the 18th Century onwards as a haven for large industry, with coal mining and shipbuilding being it's to key to prosperity.

It's during this time that Jarrow Hall was built.

A local businessman called Simon Temple built The Hall in the 1785 as a family home.

Temple was known for his extravagance with the rebuilding of Hylton Castle in Sunderland. His wealth had come from shipbuilding on the banks of the Tyne. He also brought coal mining to Jarrow when he opened The Alfred Pit in 1803.

He lived here with his wife and children until his bankruptcy in 1812. He then sold his entire estate to brothers, Thomas and Robert Brown.

Thomas moved north from London to live in the Hall with his family.

In 1841, he passed away and his son and his wife (Thomas and Isabella) inherited the estate. They lived in the Hall until 1873 when they passed away, leaving the Hall to their son Drewett.

Drewett moved away from the Hall and leased the building to Thomas Brady who moved in along with his family.

Heartbreak was to hit The Bradys, when his wife Jane died during the birth of their fifth child. Thomas continued to raise his family and three years later remarried to a local woman called Sarah Jane Wright. They lived happily together until Sarah died in 1900. Thomas lived alone again, until five years later when he married for the third time to another local called Kate Oddy. The couple moved out a year later and left the Hall empty.

It stayed empty until 1910 when owner Drewett died. He died childless and the estate was inherited by his Uncle's Grandson, Alfred Chaytor.

Alfred never lived in the building, leasing it out instead. He donated part of the grounds to the local council for it to be used as a public park, which today is still known as Drewett's Park, named in honour of the previous owner. During the early 1900's he also allowed the Hall to be used as a fever hospital.

In 1920 Alfred sold off Jarrow Hall and it had many occupants until 1935 when it was taken over by the local council. It had many uses including it being an ammunition store and gas mask centre during World War II.

By the 1970's the Hall had fallen into a state of disrepair and was only saved by The St. Paul's Development Trust who, in 1974, opened as a museum for the nearby monastery.

Since then the estate has run as a charity.

The Hall has as vast a history over the past centuries as has Jarrow itself, which is probably now most famous for The Jarrow March or Jarrow Crusade when 200 men walked to London in protest of the growing unemployment and poverty in the area due to the closing of Palmer's Shipyard.

Or the Jarra Slacks (Jarrow Slake), a tidal mudflat that runs into The Tyne.

Both of which would be well known to Jarrow's most famous resident, Star Trek's Jean Luc Picard, known locally as Patrick Stewart who spent his childhood in the town.

As you have just read Jarrow Hall and its surrounding area has a wealth of history. From the Romans to 19th Century entrepreneurs this locations' energy has excited GHOSTnortheast. From the start of our first ever investigation we were already reporting unexplained noises and events.

DIARIES OF THE INVESTIGATIONS.

Investigation #1:

We started the night with a callout in the downstairs hallway, at the bottom of the stairs in the 18th Century Hall and it wasn't long before some strange things started to happen.

As we called out, several guests reported temperature fluctuations. At first, we thought this was due to the draughts in the hall.
One gentleman started to become distressed. When asked if he was alright, he didn't answer. As we took his arm he collapsed. We removed him from the building and he improved immediately. He had no explanation for what had happened but was visibly shaken by the encounter, however this was going to be a theme of the night!

Also, during the callout, guests were reporting movement on the staircase. People were also reporting movement on the landing area above us.

We were looking in the reflection of the large window, but there did seem to be a dark figure on the floor above. It became such a talking point that one of the team and an independent guest went up the stairs to check it wasn't something natural like a piece of furniture. Both confirmed that the landing area was clear.

Upstairs Jarrow Hall:
The Hall has a vast number of rooms but we concentrated on the main bedroom area to use the Ouija board. Two of the groups did get some strong responses, with one group getting two names that were claimed to be linked to the house. As it is such a new location we will research the names we recorded, and report back at a later date.

During the experiments, again we had guests needing to leave as they either felt unwell or very uneasy.

At the back of the house is a second staircase and this the oldest part of the house.
Whilst calling out on camera, a moaning noise can clearly be heard. It does sound like a woman's voice and this is available to view on YouTube. I can corroborate there was no-one else in the area when this was recorded.
.

Cellar Jarrow Hall:
All three groups reported some very good responses on the Frank's Box in the cellar. We have received a host of names and dates for us to research to see if they are linked or just random coincidence.

This area proved too much for some of our group members.

A gentleman collapsed on two occasions and was carried out of the hall. He didn't return on the second occasion, deciding to wait for his group outside.
Two other guests came out of the cellar area not to return. Both reported feeling extremely scared and

uneasy. Both had reported being touched. The two in question were in different groups and did not know each other or each other's experiences until later.

Anglo-Saxon Settlement:

The highlight of the settlement area was one group who reported someone walking around the building.

They said that they had seen a shadow of a figure walking past the door blocking out the light.

Obviously, this led to the group becoming scared in the area as we had checked and no-one was there.

Investigation #2:

We were excited by our public return to Jarrow Hall

.

We were very happy that we had managed to squeeze in another visit before the year end and were eager to continue where we left off last month.

We started the night with a group callout in the entrance area at the bottom of the main staircase in the Hall.

Once we had established the natural ticks and bangs we started the night.

The activity seemed to start slowly before building up. Guests reported hearing breathing next to them. This included me, at one point excusing myself for heavy breathing! (This was in jest as I do breathe quite loudly).

Then the noises and movements started upstairs.
Several guests reported what they described as a head popping around the corner at the top of the stairs. This seemed to happen on numerous occasions. Also, people reported seeing the shadows above move as if someone was moving around above us.

This had me fascinated as it was the same reports as last month, yet every guest was new to the location. These reports were accompanied with the group hearing noises throughout the house.

The Cellar:
The Cellar area is accessible from a staircase from the ground floor main entrance. It splits into three small rooms that are all joined. We decided to conduct Frank's Box down there. All three groups discarded the experiment and decided to try basic calling out. This was not pre-arranged.

All groups reported several noises. Footsteps, breaths and throughout the night they were still reporting sounds of humming and music.

We had two guests from separate groups having to leave the area due to feeling uncomfortable.

One of the groups had heard footsteps and what sounded like the above door above being opened. We confirmed no-one was in this area at the time. The group said the sounds were so vivid, that they were waiting for someone to come through the door and join them. However, although they waited, no-one arrived.

Smells of body odour and bad breath were also reported by two of the group.

Village Hut:
This area seemed to freak people out the most. As it is unconnected to the main building you do have to take a short walk through the farm.

Once at the settlement you are on open ground. The most exciting activity in this area were the recording of severe EMF fluctuations.
The settlement has no electricity in the area at all!! How we were getting electric reads, never mind the fact that they were fluctuating leaves me with no natural explanation.

Two groups reported seeing shadows within the room that seemed to be moving around the building. One group had seen someone walking past the door outside. They investigated further and found no-one in the area. When they returned to the hut they once again saw a shadow pass the doorway.

Upstairs Hall:
The upstairs of the Hall is split into several rooms served by two staircases. We used the main room for our Ouija Board, although none of the groups reported anything of note.

One group reported hearing movement outside the room four times, but everytime they looked, no-one was there. The same noises of humming and distant music were reported but as of now we still have no explanation for the source.

The back staircase produced a great piece of video. We have recorded what sounds like a lady moaning in response to questions. Two independent guests and I are seen asking for a response followed by a clear moaning sound.

Conclusion:
Jarrow Hall is fast becoming one of our most active locations.

Investigation #3:

This was a team only investigation and usually I don't report from a team event.

But what was to happen with the lettered dice experiment was to leave me completely speechless!!

It has been months since the investigation and I still have no explanation what so ever!

We conducted the letter dice experiment upstairs in The Hall. After several random words, we weren't holding out much hope of the experiment going anywhere.

Then we asked, "Who do you work for, how do you make a living?"

The dice spelled "Coal Board?" That was a nine-letter answer from 13 dice.

I followed with, "If you worked for the coal board give me a name of your employer or a name of note?" The dice spelled out "Jarrow Coke."

This was 10 letters from 13, and both answers were directly linked to the location and questions I asked. Again, this was recorded live on Facebook.

What also seemed unexplainable is the fact that Bede's Museum and Jarrow Hall are built upon Jarrow Coke Works.

I am not able to work out the odds of these answers (for which I would probably need a mathematician!) but can say I have not had these words appear in seven years of paranormal investigations.

Investigation #4

We returned to Jarrow Hall for our first visit of the year.

This is a new location but I must say the amount of information and activity we have gathered already is quite staggering.

Our Livelinks from this location have been some of the best we have broadcast so far. However, with the amount of history in the area we should not be surprised.

We started the night with our group callout in The Oval Room upstairs.

We did have to rule out a lot of the noises as natural, as the room does have quite a creaky wood floor. But before long we were reporting activity in the room that we couldn't explain.

Several guests mentioned temperature drops and feeling cold, and we cannot rule out natural drafts as there is a chimney and windows in this room, but the reports did not seem to follow what would be natural.

One guest reported cold on the front of her face, however the window was behind of her. This was also the case with two other reports that said the cold was on the front of their body, when the natural draught was at the back of them.

Thuds and movement were reported outside on the stairwell when there was no-one there. A report of figure in one of the doorways left us wondering. At first, we thought it was a shadow from the guests, but the shadowy figure didn't move when we asked the group to move. Also in this area one of the group had reported that they had gone extremely hot to the point of having to leave the circle to remove their jumper. The temperature logger, showed the room stayed at 10 degrees. The member of the group next to her folded over in pain. He asked to leave as he described the pain as feeling as if someone had hit him the "nether regions". Interestingly, he had had to leave the room on a previous visit after feeling discomfort in the same room. Unsurprisingly he didn't return to the room for the rest of the night.

Upstairs:

As the groups split up we used The Oval Room for our Ouija Board experiment.

Nobody reported much activity and turned their attentions to other experiments. One group had a very successful dice session.

During the session, the group had "Alice" and "Burn" come through on the lettered dice. The group questioned further thinking the "Burn" could mean how she had died. Unknown to them at the time that one of the ladies who lived in the hall in 1801 until her death was called "Alice Burn."

The dice are completely random and cannot be manipulated in anyway, so we can only explain it as paranormal or sheer coincidence.

The LiveLink from the rear staircase recorded some interesting activity. A lady's scream can be clearly heard on the broadcast; it sounds distant and we checked with entire group and no-one else on the estate heard the scream, ruling out any noise pollution. A few minutes later, we recorded a noise that sounded like something metallic being thrown.

The broadcast is still available unedited on our Facebook group.

Anglo-Saxon Settlement:
We use the K-2 and EMF Meters in this area as there is no electricity and we are in a remote area of the location. We also insist that all mobile phones are switched to their flight modes to ensure no interference.

One group recorded activity on both meters. The meters seem to move to response and answered questions. During a session, we had sat a gentleman in the main chair. From questions and responses on the meters we moved him and replaced him with a young lady.

The meters response answered that the lady reminded him of us wife, at this point one of the gentleman in our group become very emotional, saying he wanted to cry. When asking if the spirit was doing this both meters responded.

During a similar session one of the groups reported that the meters were responding to children, especially a small girl. This has been reported at every previous visit.

Conclusion:

I could have filled another two pages with the information we received on this investigation. What is interesting is the data that we are gathering is starting to see repeats on every visit, with the same names involved.

Investigation #5

The team headed just South of the Tyne Tunnel to the newly opened Jarrow Hall.

Although the daytime had seen downpours that had flooded parts of Jarrow and the nearby South Shields, the night had become dry and clear if not a little chilly.

Again, the night was not going to disappoint. Even after only six months of investigations, Jarrow Hall is becoming one of the most active locations I have experienced since founding GHOSTnortheast.

We started the night with a group callout at the

bottom of the main staircase.

We hadn't even finished our blessing when noises were being heard from upstairs and down the hallway. It took us four attempts to finish our blessing, as if someone didn't want us doing it.

Once the calling out started, several of the guests were reporting hearing voices and footsteps behind them. Others reported heavy breathing. The group all heard noises coming from the upstairs rooms. These were so distinct that we had to stop while we sent someone upstairs to make sure the area was clear. They confirmed no-one was there.

As we continued the calling out, a few guests started to report feeling very cold on various parts of their bodies. One guest had to leave the building after feeling extremely ill. Interestingly, they had stood in the exact same place as guests that have left on two previous investigations.

The guest then returned, but only lasted a matter of minutes before being removed again. This guest would leave after only half an hour of the investigation as she said she just could not do it! She has been with us before so knew what to expect from the night, but the experience had shaken her up and she felt that she needed to leave.

A figure was reported at the end of the hallway by

several guests. All of them described the same thing and were all in agreement on its movement. At the same time, a shadow was reported at the top of the staircase.

At one part of the callout, everyone seemed to be talking at the same time, as everyone was experiencing something!

The Cellar:

The Cellar was to become too intense for some of our guests.

In one group a particular guest became very unnerved by her surroundings, to the point where she was visibly shaking and started to cry, yet she could give no reason for feeling this way. We asked if she wanted to leave the location but she persevered.

Later, with another group, two of the guests became overcome in the area and had to sit in our Hub area until the group finished. Again, they could give no explanation for these feelings.

One of the groups reported the temperature of the room changing dramatically. One moment they were hot in the area, then in the next moment the room went really cold. This fluctuated several times during they time in the area. Later we examined our data logger and it confirmed the temperature spikes but we have no explanation as it only happened during this group's time there.

Anglo-Saxon Settlement:

Two of the groups reported several fluctuations of the EMF and K-2 meters in this area. We find this very strange as there is no electricity near this part of the location, so we can rule out any natural causes.

Guests also reported seeing figures in this area. One groups explanation was that when the light was off it felt as if the room was crowded and the benches seemed full. But when the light was switched back on, they couldn't believe how far apart they were from other guests.

Upstairs of The Hall:

Nothing of note was reported on the Ouija Board from any of the groups. And although we did get words on the lettered dice, nothing was of significance and couldn't be ruled out by mere coincidence.

Noises were recorded around this area which did seem to continue from the original call out.

Investigation #6

It had been raining earlier in the day but the evening had become sunny and dry. The night was warm and there was no wind. We did have the light of a full moon.

We gathered in the downstairs stairwell of the Hall to start the night with a group callout.

During the callout, guests at the bottom of the area reported hearing toilets being flushed. When we looked in the toilets which are located further down the hallway there was no-one to be seen. Both the gentlemen's and lady's toilets where empty and the toilets were dry. So, we had heard water flushing but there was no evidence to suggest that they had been flushed. A few minutes later the guests reported hearing running water, like taps being switched on. Again, we visited the toilets and there was nothing to be seen. This activity seemed to last the whole duration of the group callout and we have no explanation for what was happening.

One guest had to leave the investigation after she felt tightening around the throat which was making her cough. It got too uncomfortable for her and she spent time outside. This is third time this happened to the person that stands next to the doorway.

As the callout moved on, several guests reported seeing things on the stairs. One guest was chosen to sit on the stairs.

She reported feeling like someone was next to her and felt as if it was a child. During the time, she was reporting these feelings, the remaining guests were reporting her head and face going very dark. At one point, we could not see her features or hair. It was reported that it was as if she had a black cloth over her head.

Several noises were heard upstairs and an independent guest walked the hall with a team member to prove there was no-one upstairs in the building during our callout!

We brought the group callout to an end and split up into smaller groups to continue the night.

The Anglo-Saxon Settlement:
One group reported physical activity in this area. During their callout in the Saxon House, the team said that they clearly heard stones being thrown across the room. As they were trying to experiment with the EMF and K-2, the group screamed as something was thrown across the room towards them. The team immediately switched on their torches, but they couldn't identify what had been

thrown.

Also in this area, we recorded many fluctuations on the EMF Meters. This is very interesting as there is no electricity in the area and every base test we have run for the past year has shown zero reads. We cannot explain this activity but it repeats every time.

The Cellar:

Unfortunately, due to the warm weather, none of the teams lasted long in the cellar due to the heat. They all went upstairs to ground floor.

Whilst on the bottom of the stairs, one group have filmed the hair of a guest getting moved to request. At the same time, some very unusual light anomalies or orbs can be seen appearing next to the lady. We will be releasing the videoed footage on YouTube as soon as we have investigated the orbs.

Also, while this activity was happening, the front door of the hall opened and closed. The team was expecting someone to walk into the hall, but no-one appeared? Everyone heard the noise of the door.

The door in question is a heavy front door and is not affected by drafts etc. We have no explanation to what opened the door!

Upstairs:

We used the Ouija board but no-one reported much

activity.

The dice were more successful as a name appeared which we have reported 3 times before. The name which is both forename and surname is a direct link to the Hall.

Conclusion:

As with previous visits, I could have filled more space with what had happened tonight.

Jarrow Hall keeps delivering unexplainable activity and repeats the same information repeatedly.

11 THE THEATRE ROYAL
NEWCASTLE-UPON-TYNE

It must be one of the most iconic buildings in the North East and one of the most recognised landmarks after the Tyne Bridge in Newcastle.

The Theatre Royal stands on the world-famous Grey Street, which has been voted the most beautiful street in the world on numerous occasions, and is a fine example of 19th Century architecture at its best.
But as always, I will start the research on the land that it's built.

The back of the building stands on Pilgrim Street and would have been part of the Monastery that stood in Newcastle nearly 2000 years ago that unfortunately caught fire and killed many of the Novocastrian Monks that lived and worked there. We can't be certain but we think The Theatre Royal stands

197

roughly where the farm and stables were built.

The Monastery served the Pilgrims that would travel across the Tyne to visit Jesmond and then up to Lindisfarne, hence the name "Pilgrim Street".

Moving further forward in time, the building would have stood in the grounds of 16th Century Mansion House that stood on the site of The Franciscan Friar; This was called "The Newe House".

When King Charles I was captured by the Scots in 1646, he was held as a prisoner in The Newe House until his release in 1647.

The Manor was owned by Sir Francis Anderson until 1675, when he sold it to Sir Thomas Blackett. The Blacketts were to own the land for over a Century until it was sold to a local master builder called George Anderson in 1783.

His son Major Anderson later renamed the area Anderson Place and he later donated the six-ton bell to St. Nicholas' Cathedral. This was named "The Major Bell" and still rings across the city today.

After his death in 1834 the 12-acre site was sold to Richard Grainger for little over £45,000.

Once Grainger had the site, he developed plans for redevelopment. The City's Corporation were hesitant to allow the building project due to the vast areas of open land.

However, due to the quality of Grainger's previous work at Old Eldon Square and The Royal Arcade, the public signed a 5000-strong petition and The Corporation allowed the work to begin. During the project, Grainger had to demolish the butcher's Market and the original Theatre Royal that stood on Moseley Street with the agreement he had to rebuild the theatre for the people.

During the next 5 years Newcastle City Centre was transformed.

Over 700 workmen removed over 5 million cubic feet of earth to create nine streets that still stand today. The most impressive and splendid being "Grey Street".

Grainger employed local architects John and Benjamin Green. The pair were also known for local building The Lit and Phil Library, Grey's Monument and Penshaw Monument in Sunderland.

Grainger explained that he wanted The Theatre to be the centre of his grand design for Newcastle.

And on the 20th of February in 1837 the doors opened for the first time at "The Theatre Royal".

The Merchant of Venice was it's very first production. The Theatre became an instant hit but unfortunately after a performance of Macbeth in 1899, tragedy struck the grand building.

The fire destroyed the interior of the theatre and it had to be re-designed. A man called Frank Matcham was commissioned with the work to bring the building back to its former glory. Indeed, the current theatre's restaurant, "Matchams" was named after him. Luckily the exterior of the building was undamaged and the frontage of this fantastic Grade I building still looks exactly the same to this day.

The interior construction took nearly two years to complete but finally the theatre re-opened on 31st of December 1901.

Over the years The Theatre had some restoration projects notably during the late Eighties.

In March 2011, the Theatre went dark. For the first time since the great fire The Theatre Royal closed its doors to be completely restored and expanded so it could house modern performances. It re-opened its doors in September 2011 with a performance of "The Madness of George III". Fittingly, it was King George the third was who gave The Theatre it's Royal Charter.

As with most theatres The Royal is no different for having its share of ghost stories.

A grey lady has often been reported in the upper circle. It is believed that she jumped to her death after being spurned by her lover.

Monks have been reported in the area, with footsteps in the back corridors and noises on the stage when no-one is around.

Where do we investigate?
We investigate most areas of The Theatre, but we don't have access to the Dressing Rooms for obvious reasons.

However, the main auditorium and under the stage have delivered some extremely interesting results.

The public bar areas have also seen some questionable results as the answers all seem to link together.

During a team only investigation, two of our team saw a figure moving around in the Grand Circle.

Both described seeing a person moving around the seats then into the aisle. After calling out several times with no response they sent another team member down to see who was in the area as they thought it was one of the Theatre staff.

No-one was found in the area and all team members and staff were accounted for.

On our first public night, all three groups reported footsteps above them when they were under the stairs. These were separate reports at different times and all three groups did not know what the previous groups had reported. On all three occasions we had cameras recording the stage and show nobody in this area when the footsteps are heard.

One of the doors in the Auditorium opened and slammed shut on numerous occasions during our nights; We have investigated natural causes such as drafts or faults with the door and couldn't give a natural reason. This activity has also been reported in the past by staff of The Theatre and seems to be a regular occurrence.

Conclusion:
The Theatre Royal certainly has the history and the reputation for being haunted.

However, as we have just added this location to our portfolio we haven't had enough time to fully investigate it's strange goings on.

Over the next few months as we revisit this fantastic

building, hopefully we will build a full report.

The first couple of visits have proven fruitful with some very unusual activity.

I was witness to the figure moving around in the Grand Circle and we still can't find a rational explanation to who it was.

DIARIES OF THE INVESTIGATIONS.

Investigation #1

Tonight, took us back to Newcastle's City Centre for us to investigate our second new location and probably one of the most iconic buildings on Newcastle's famous Grey Street.

We gathered in the main auditorium for the start of the night. As we called out we heard some unexplained noises coming from the stage area. The far fire exit door sounded as if it had opened but it was a windy night and we can't rule out natural causes due to the building being old. We did get reports from several guests of seeing a figure in one of the private boxes that looked as if it kept leaning forward to see us. Again, on further investigation there was no-one in the area.

Under Stage and Stalls:
One of our guests reported seeing someone coming down the stage right steps whilst under the stage. She described seeing legs but then no-one was there. We investigated further but no-one could be found. Another group were under the stage and reported hearing footsteps crossing the stage above from left to right and when they waited for someone to come down the steps no-one appeared. Was this a mere

coincidence? However, as you read on you will see how often stage right is mentioned.

In the Stalls, two groups reported hearing a door opening. It seemed to be the same door from earlier in the callout. Again, we watched this door for drafts but we were unable to draw a conclusion.

Harrison Room:

In this area, we used the Planchette. Two of the groups both had what looked like a triangle and a L shape drawn side by side.

I can confirm neither group saw what had been drawn by the other. We don't know the relevance of these shapes but it is highly unusual that two completely separate groups would draw the same thing? One other group kept getting a "S" and "R" drawn. Does it mean Stage Right?

Third Floor Bar Area:

Frank's Box was used in this part of the location with our lettered dice. All three groups have reported in their notes the words "stage" and "right" although not in one sentence. They all recorded the word "fell" several times.

The dice words overall looked random but again all three groups have highlighted the word fell and one

group had "falling."
The last group in this area recorded the dice spelling "Stager," and dismissed it as unimportant.

However, when I read this whilst writing this report I have read it as "Stage R." Is this another coincidence or am I reading more into something that isn't there?

Conclusion:
A great opening night at a fantastic location. I think we have haven't even scratched the surface of this huge building.

The amount of times stage right and the word fell were noted is highly unusual for one night and when you look at all three group reports together it is quite staggering at how similar they are. I'm looking forward to an encore and repeat performance at The Theatre Royal, Newcastle.

Investigation #2

What a great location to start the Autumn/Winter Season.

We were in the middle of our hometown at one of its most iconic buildings for only the second public paranormal investigation at The Theatre Royal.

This 150 years old building has a wealth of stories attached and we were not going to be disappointed with the activity we would witness.

We started the night in the main auditorium and stood in the Stalls for our traditional group call-out. Almost immediately we were reporting noises around The Theatre.

At first, we seem to hear footsteps and shuffling in the Circle above us.

This was then replaced with noises downstairs near us.

After we heard what sounded like footsteps to the left of us, the fire door opened and slammed shut. Everyone witnessed it in the group. When we investigated further, there was nobody there. Also, it is worth noting that this is a fire door and is heavy, so we can rule out any draughts or breezes. Interestingly it was in the area of stage right, which is significant to our previous investigation in February.

After everyone had calmed down, guests were reporting temperature drops and breezes around them, as if someone was moving between them.

A lady's voice was also reported in this area but it could not be heard on any of the recordings we made.

We then split up into separate groups to investigate the location in full.

The Harrison Room:
We used our Planchette experiment in this room and had mixed results. One group had some fantastic activity. The planchette seemed to be answering questions with yes and no answers; Then the Teamleader then played some show tunes on their phone only to see the planchette bounding in tune.

We have recorded this and watched in back and although it sounds daft, it looks like the planchette is dancing around the page. I have further investigated the recording and can verify that all guests were using their finger nails, so I can't see manipulation to the equipment.

Other groups in this location did record names and dates that are associated with The Theatre; I have recorded them to see if they become relevant at further investigations.

The Main Auditorium/Under the Stage:
After the start of the night, we were optimistic for the rest of the night but unfortunately it wasn't as active as we hoped. Although one group did witness the doors opening again during their call out sessions. A few guests did report movement around the stage

area but we could not find anybody there when we looked closer.

Under the stage several guests reported that they had been touched.

Also, there were reports of the feeling of children running around in this area.

Again, as with our last investigation, we recorded several noises of movement above us on stage. We can 100% guarantee that no-one was above us at it was sealed off due to the preparations for the arrival of the Mary Poppins show.

As with last time the movement revolved around "Stage Right".

Upper Floor/Gallery Seating:
We used the Frank's Box and lettered dice in this area and became unexplainable was the number of times we received the word "stab" or "stabbed".

This again is a replica of our last investigation here. Are we missing something in The Theatre Royal's history?

One group had swearing across the radio on several occasions and when they pushed for further activity, one of the windows started to shake. This could be heard as well as seen.

I can't rule out a natural breeze has caused this to happen but it is quite surprising that it only happened once and coincided with the questioning at the time.

All three groups reported the same name and a particular year through the box. I'm currently researching both to see if I can find any information that is connected to the location.

Conclusion:

The Theatre Royal is a magnificent building with many stories to tell. It is an honour to be the paranormal group to gain access to see what hides behind the curtain after hours.

I added it at the end of this book as it is a brand new location and we haven't had a lot of time in the location, but due to the amount of unexplained activity I thought I would share what we have found so far.

11 CONCLUSION

This book only scratches the surface of the activity we have encountered over the past seven years and I have only featured a third of the locations that we have investigated.

I hope as you have read through our investigations you will have noted how much repeat activity we get. The same thing but on different nights, at different times and with different people.

We have hours of video tape and hundreds of photographs that we constantly look through from each investigation and we are still finding activity that we cannot explain.

People ask me if I believe in ghosts? I really don't know. Over the years I have certainly seen, heard and felt some unusual things, but what they are, I'm just not sure. Is it nature playing tricks? Is it The Afterlife?

I just don't have the answers. I suppose the day I do will be the day I stop looking.

What I say at all our nights is that I'm not here to change anyone's opinion or belief, as I can't prove or disprove the existence of ghosts or past life.

I can only present the information that we find and the rest is for you to decide.

I think the best quote that sums things up for me is one from Arthur Conan Doyle;

"*Once you eliminate the impossible, whatever remains, no matter how improbable, must be the truth.*"

STEVE WATSON

ABOUT THE AUTHOR

Steve Watson has worked in the Retail Sector for over 25 years and is currently a manager in a local department store.
His past includes a short time in The RAF.

He has investigated the paranormal for over thirty years and has a vast knowledge on the local history of the North East.
This is the first book on his experiences.

He is married with two children and lives on Tyneside.

CONTACTS:

Website: www.GHOSTnortheast.co.uk

E-mail: info@ghostnortheast.co.uk

YouTube: www.youtube.com/Ghostnortheast

Follow us on Facebook and Twitter

STEVE WATSON

Cover Design by DBF

The Little Theatre Photograph used with the kind

Printed in Great Britain
by Amazon

10790022R00129